Overcoming
Anxiety

Overcoming Anxiety

Gary R. Collins

Vision
House
Santa Ana, California 92705

To Julie, Marilynn, and Janice

OVERCOMING ANXIETY
Formerly published as
A PSYCHOLOGIST LOOKS AT LIFE
Revised edition copyright © 1973
VISION HOUSE PUBLISHERS
Santa Ana, California 92705
ISBN 0-87801-017-3
Printed in U.S.A.

Contents

Preface
1. ANXIETY 11
2. DISCOURAGEMENT 30
3. ANGER 46
4. GUILT 60
5. INFERIORITY 76
6. PRIDE 94
7. ENVY 106
8. LONELINESS 119
9. BUSYNESS 131
10. EMPTINESS 145

ACKNOWLEDGMENTS

For permission to reprint excerpts in this book, grateful acknowledgment is made to the following publishers:

The Bobbs-Merrill Company, Inc.—for excerpts from Eugene E. Levitt's *The Psychology of Anxiety,* copyright © 1967.

Christianity Today—for excerpts from John R. W. Stott's "When Should a Christian Weep?" November 7, 1969.

Conservative Baptist Press—for excerpts from Leslie B. Flynn's *You Can Live Above Envy,* copyright © 1970.

Doubleday & Company, Inc.—for excerpts from Theodore Roszak's *The Making of a Counter Culture,* copyright © 1968.

Eternity—for reproduction of Roberta J. Johnson's "Our Church's Prayer," copyright © 1966, The Evangelical Foundation, 1716 Spruce Street, Philadelphia, Pa.

Harper & Row Publishers—for excerpts from Erich Fromm's *The Heart of Man,* copyright © 1964; Edward B. Lindaman's *Space: A New Direction for Mankind,* copyright © 1969; and Snell Putney and Gail J. Putney's *The Adjusted American: Normal Neurosis in the Individual and Society,* copyright © 1964.

Inter-Varsity Press—for excerpts from Charles E. Hummel's *Tyranny of the Urgent,* copyright © 1967.

Tyndale House Publishers—for excerpts from Richard Wolff's *Man at the Top,* copyright © 1969; and John D. Jess, *Escape from Emptiness,* copyright © 1968.

Washington Square Press—for excerpts from V. E. Frankl's *Man's Search for Meaning: An Introduction to Logotherapy,* copyright © 1959.

The Westminister Press—for excerpts from Wayne E. Oates' *Anxiety in Christian Experience,* copyright © 1955, W. L. Jenkins.

Word Books—for excerpts from Keith Miller's *The Taste of New Wine,* copyright © 1965.

Zondervan Publishing House—for excerpts from Billy Graham's *The Seven Deadly Sins,* copyright © 1955.

Preface

What is life?

Is it no more than a tale told by an idiot, full of sound and fury, signifying nothing?

Is it only a vapor that passes away? Or can it be something abundant?

Must it be limited to a few years on this earth? Or does it continue in some other form after death?

These questions are as old as recorded history. Ancient philosophers asked them. So did the Biblical writers and the great poets. So do people today—people worried about world famine, over-population, environmental pollution and nuclear warfare. People of all ages, but especially the young, wonder about purpose in life and the meaning of our existence. Some seek answers in science, others look to cults, astrology, eastern religions, or the message of a spiritual guru. Some have dropped out of this world and entered one of promiscuous sex and drug-induced escapism. Middle-class suburbia is going through life on the installment plan, struggling to get ahead in the world, drifting from one aquisition to the next. But in spite of all this sound and fury, many people—including those who are firmly involved in established churches—find life confusing and empty, signifying nothing.

Apparently man can neither understand nor control himself. The triumphs of space exploration accentuate the irony that it is easier for man to go to the moon than to wipe out a slum; easier for him to ride through space than to clean up his own polluted skies; easier for him to manage cooperation in a vast business enterprise than to mold brotherhood in a city block.[1]

---

[1] Lindaman, E. B., *Space, A New Direction For Mankind.* New York: Harper & Row, 1969 (on book jacket).

In the chapters of this book I have attempted to take a close look at life, with all of its emotions and complexities. Our attention will be focused not on the world of outer space but on the inner emotions of man; not on how we can conquer the universe but on how we can conquer and control ourselves. In approaching the aspects of life that are discussed in the following pages I have been guided by three considerations: my personal observations as a clinical psychologist, a review of the contemporary psychological literature, and a consideration of what the Bible says about man and his emotions. By combining the findings of modern psychology with the truths of Scripture, I have tried to produce a book which is both informative and of practical value to those who want to *overcome anxiety* and live more effectively.

Perceptive and helpful comments from a number of people have formed the material which appears in the following pages. Portions of this manuscript have been presented verbally and the response of listeners has been of great help as the material was rewritten and revised. In addition, each of the chapters was discussed in detail during a graduate seminar at Trinity Evangelical Divinity School.

I am especially grateful for the helpful suggestions of Fred Lutz, Richard Meyers, Loren Pine, J. David Crockett, and David Busby. And with her usual efficiency, Carol Kiehlbauch deciphered my handwriting and typed the manuscript. Then, once again, my wife Julie gave both encouragement and helpful suggestions. The life that she lives as a wife, a mother, and a follower of Jesus Christ is a constant encouragement that helps me to overcome my own anxieties.

Mundelein, Illinois   *G.R.C.*

CHAPTER 1

Anxiety

It is the official emotion of our age, the most pervasive psychological phenomenon of our time, fully understood by no one, the central problem in understanding and treating mental illness. This is what psychologists and psychiatrists say about anxiety.[1] Some have suggested we are living in an Age of Anxiety, when everything we do is colored by this universal emotion. One such writer has concluded that "the 20th century is more anxiety-ridden than any other era in history since the Middle Ages."[2]

There are various reasons for this prevalence of anxiety in this last third of the 20th century. Modern technology is producing such rapid and far-reaching changes in our standards of living that some people become anxious simply trying to keep up. In addition, the mass media have made it possible for us immediately to be aware of the problems that are going on in the world around us. The tensions in the Middle and Far East; our troubled economy; exploding campuses; pollution; over-population; hunger; tension in the ghettos; crime and civil disobedience; the increasing ability of scientists to manipulate and control human behavior; the changing values of youth; and a host of other issues are constantly bombarding us. Is it any wonder modern man feels anxious?

But anxiety is familiar even to those who somehow manage to ignore the daily news. Many of us feel anxious when we go to the dentist, when we take a driver's test, when we contract an undiagnosed illness, when we find ourselves in constantly changing situations. So common is anxiety that it touches virtually all of us and leads to untold tension and misery.

In this first chapter we will discuss what anxiety is, how it affects people, what causes it, how it can be handled, and the attitudes which Christians should have toward anxiety and worry.

The Meaning of Anxiety

Anxiety is an emotion which is characterized by feelings of apprehension, dread, uneasiness, worry, or concern and which is accompanied by physical arousal (increased pulse, perspiration, etc.).

When a person has anxious feelings, he is usually concerned about some possible danger, problem, or embarrassment. When we feel anxious about teaching a Sunday school class or giving a speech, for example, we are apprehensive lest we make a fool of ourselves, say something wrong, do something that might be embarrassing or forget what we intended to say.

The little child who is anxious in the presence of a big dog feels his apprehension over the possibility that the dog may knock him over, bite him, bark at him, or otherwise hurt or disturb his well-being.

Psychological studies show that the feeling can vary. First, anxious feelings can be either *specific* or *free-floating*. Specific anxiety results when we are consciously aware of some threatening situation or object. Claustrophobia, for example, is a specific anxiety which arises because the person has a fear of being in tight spaces. Others feel anxious about height, traveling on water or the presence of snakes.

Several years ago my wife and I invited a friend to visit our home and stay overnight with the family. Shortly before everyone settled down for the night, our guest asked if he could bring his pet inside the house. We agreed, only to discover that the pet was a six-foot boa constrictor! Understandably my wife began to feel a little anxious and insecure. This was a specific anxiety. She knew why she was apprehensive and what was bothering her.

This specific kind of anxiety is quite common. The anxious person is clearly aware of what is troubling him, and is both apprehensive about what might happen and about his inability to act appropriately.

In contrast to this is free-floating anxiety. Here the person does not know why he feels as he does. He is afraid something terrible is going to happen but what it is or what he can do about it is a mystery to him.

While specific and free-floating anxiety are both seen in our society (and to some extent are present in each of us), specific anxiety is more the common problem while free-floating anxiety tends to characterize highly troubled persons.

Anxiety can also be either *acute* or *chronic*. An acute condition is one which comes quickly, is of high intensity, and of short duration—like acute appendicitis. In contrast, a chronic condition is of lower intensity but lasts for a much longer time—like a chronic heart condition.

Some people are chronically crippled by an anxiety which is persistent and long-lasting. But just as some people are more accident prone than others, so some are more *anxiety* prone.

In contrast, most of us experience anxiety in more acute, intense fashions. Some situation comes along which makes us feel anxious for a time but as soon as the perceived danger passes the anxiety disappears also.

Sigmund Freud was the first to make a distinction between *normal* and *neurotic* anxiety. Normal anxiety occurs when there is real danger and when it makes sense to be anxious. When the astronauts on the Apollo 12 moon journey had trouble with their spaceship and were in danger of being lost in space, apprehension was quite natural and normal.

On the other hand, neurotic, abnormal anxiety involves intense feelings of discomfort when danger is mild or even non-existent. (It isn't always easy to distinguish between neurotic and normal anxiety—even Freud recognized this—and sometimes it all depends on whose point of view you arc taking. For instance, our house guest knew a great deal about "Boris," his boa constrictor, and believed the "pet" was harmless. From his perspective, anxiety in the presence of his snake might have been neurotic, but from my wife's point of view, anxiety was quite normal. She saw the snake as a dangerous creature and felt uncomfortable in its presence.)

Regardless of the kind of anxiety one feels, physical reactions always come with it. Some of these reactions we can easily recognize. Discomfort in our stomach ("butterflies"), a tightness in the throat ("a lump"), dryness in the mouth, a rapid heartbeat, shortness of breath, inability to sleep, a loss of appetite, and a frequent desire to urinate are all conscious reactions to anxiety. Other physical responses are not so easily recognized. These include changes in our blood pressure, a slowing of digestive processes, general tension, or changes in the chemical composition of the blood. And it is possible for a person's hair to stand on end in times of anxiety, for "goose bumps" to develop on the skin, or for the person to blanch with fear.

These physical reactions harm us only if they persist. When this happens, the body eventually yields under the pressure. Stomach ulcers, intense headaches, high blood pressure, and other physical ailments often occur directly as a result of persistent anxiety.

The Effects of Anxiety

How do people act when anxious? Numerous researchers have studied this question[3] and some of their findings are summarized in Figure 1-1. When anxiety is low or non-existent, people are often poorly motivated. Life is dull, boring, inefficient and unsatisfying. Very much anxiety, however, is worse. It interferes with learning, adversely affects our memory (what happens in stage fright), hinders performance of skills, interferes with problem solving and blocks effective communication. As shown on the right of the diagram, our efficiency is also low when we are highly anxious. There is also great dissatisfaction and frustration with life.

Several years ago psychologist Irving Janis did an interesting study of surgical patients.[4] In order to see how much anxiety was present he interviewed a number of these patients a few hours before surgery. On the basis of these interviews he was able to divide the patients into three groups. The non-anxious patients were cheerful and optimistic about their impending operations. They denied feeling worried about the surgery, slept well the night before, watched TV and joked freely in the hours prior to the operation. Moderately anxious patients were outwardly calm and apparently not obsessed with the coming operation, but they wanted information about the surgeon's procedures, needed reassurance, and admitted to feeling some tension. People in the third group, the highly anxious patients, were constantly worry-

Figure 1-1.

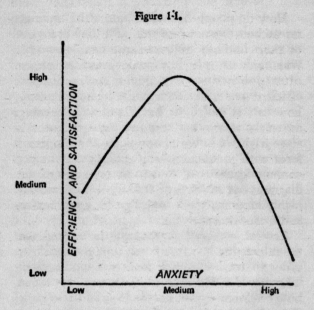

The Effects of Anxiety. When anxiety is low, efficiency and satisfaction with life are low. Efficiency and satisfaction are also low when there is high anxiety. When a medium amount of anxiety is present, efficiency of behavior and general satisfaction with life are both high.

ing and jittery as they faced surgery. Reassurance about the operation did little to calm them down. They couldn't sleep the night before and were worried about medical complications and possible death.

After the surgery these three groups of patients were interviewed again. The moderately anxious patients showed the quickest recovery and the best post-operative morale. They were able to tolerate the discomfort of drainage tubes, injections, or nausea, and they recovered most quickly. In contrast those people who had very high or very low anxiety before surgery showed slower recovery, poorer morale, inability to get along with others, an increased tendency to criticize, and both a fear and an intolerance of treatment. From this the psychologist concluded people function best when they approach surgery with some moderate amount of anxiety.

Once again, it is hard to define and measure "a moderate amount of anxiety." What may be good for one person may not be good for another. But a moderate amount of anxiety (not too little and not too much) is healthy and desirable. In the words of one psychologist, when anxiety is in small doses and appropriately handled, it "is not in and of itself abnormal, unhealthy, or even necessarily bad. . . .(It is) part and parcel of normal human life."[5]

These findings have many practical implications. In medicine, as we have seen above, patients recover best when they have an average amount of anxiety. In counseling it appears some anxiety in the counselee is good. In education, including Christian education, the person who is paralyzed by anxiety and the person who has no anxiety whatsoever do not learn nearly as well as the person who has an average amount.

The Causes of Anxiety

Why is anxiety so common? Dr. Ernest R. Hilgard, past president of the American Psychological Association and a distinguished psychologist, has suggested one answer:

> The causes of contemporary anxiety are complex: Two world wars within our century, and a cold war persisting since the last one; enormous mobilities of peoples, geographically and economically, disturbing the sense of rootedness; shifting values so that we are uncertain about child-rearing practices, about moral standards, about religious beliefs.[6]

This does not say, however, why children are anxious with a strange babysitter, why many adults are anxious in the presence of snakes, why numerous committed Christians are so anxious about sharing their faith that they remain silent except for rationalizing that they "don't want to offend anybody."

There are at least four reasons why people become anxious.

First, we learn by experience to be anxious. Most people have heard of the experiments with dogs by Pavlov conducted in Russia almost a century ago. In one of these experiments Pavlov rang a bell, immediately following this with a mild electric shock to the animal's back leg. Before long the dog showed signs of anxiety whenever the bell rang. Clearly the animal had learned that the bell signalled something painful, and thus the bell sound became anxiety arousing. When I was a young child we lived near a lake and my grandfather used to take me to watch excursion boats come into port. While I enjoyed watching the hustle and bustle of passengers boarding and leaving these vessels, the sight of the boats also made me feel anxious because I knew that invariably someone on the bridge would blow the whistle. As a little boy the noise of that whistle scared me, and once I associated the boat with the noise I became anxious whenever the ship sailed up to the dock. Also, if you have ever taken a driver's test and failed it, you know what it is to learn by experience to be anxious. When a person takes the test and fails, he associates the test situation with the pain of failure. Then, when he goes to take his test next time, he is anxious because of what he has learned through past experience.

A second cause of anxiety is the example shown by other people. Children learn to be anxious by watching parents and other adults. The mother who is anxious at the time of a thunderstorm, for example, conveys her anxiety to the child, who later becomes anxious in the same situation. Highly anxious parents almost invariably have highly anxious children.

Socialization is the third cause of anxiety. By "socialization" we mean the process by which a child learns and adopts to the standards and ways of his society. Almost from the day of birth, parents—and later teachers and other adults—put limitations on a child and establish rules so that the young person will be trained in the way that he should go. To assure this conformity, adults reward the child's behavior when it is desirable, withhold something he wants when the behavior is unacceptable, and punish undesirable behavior. The child is also threatened. Misbehave, we say, and you will be spanked, sent to your room, not permitted to have your dessert, or deprived in some other way. These threats help mold the child, but they also teach him to be anxious. Anxiety therefore may be taught along with the rules of society. "Theories and evidence agree anxiety is an inevitable by-product of the process by which a person learns to become a member of a society.... All basic anxiety is," in the opinion of one writer, "socialization anxiety."[7]

Fourthly, anxiety comes as we learn to think. A little child wanders into a busy street without fear because he has not yet learned to appreciate the danger of the situation. While his parents may watch television and anxiously learn of civil strife and economic tensions in the society, the childs plays happily on the floor because he has not yet learned to understand the meaning of the newscaster's words. Panic, an extreme form of anxiety, is only felt when trapped people realize the danger of a situation, recognize the importance of escaping, and appreciate the difficulty of getting out. Learning to think can also lead to anxiety over morals. Once we learn what is right and wrong we can understand the implications of our actions. This may cause us to become anxious when we are tempted to sin or anxious after we have sinned, since we then are faced with our own frailties and the threat of punishment. This anxiety over morals is at the basis of much guilt.

Another cause of anxiety has been proposed by Freud and those who stress the importance of unconscious irrational influences in a person's life. If we consciously thought about all that could harm us or could adversely influence our society, we would probably be immobilized with fear and insecurity. To prevent this, our brain manages to ignore a lot of the potential stresses and automatically to push these "out of our minds" and into what Freud called the unconscious. Thus many of our concerns and threats get lodged someplace in the brain where we don't consciously think about them. The anxiety-arousing issues are still present, the realizations of potential danger are still there, but we don't ponder these consciously. At times, however, they still produce anxiety of a free-floating type; an anxiety caused not by conscious thinking but by unconscious influences.

Coping With Anxiety

When a person gets hungry, cold or tired, he takes action to meet the problem. He raids the refrigerator, takes a nap, turns up the heat, or in some way meets his physical needs. As we go through life, we also learn how to deal with mental turmoil and conflict. When we start to feel anxious, usually we don't just sit and hope that the anxiety will go away by itself any more than we hope that hunger will take care of itself. Instead, as we mature, we discover ways in which we can handle or cope with anxiety and defend ourselves against being overwhelmed by anxious feelings. Automatically and often without consciously thinking about it, we behave in ways that enable us to deal with our anxiety and to protect ourselves against it.[8]

One of these ways of coping with anxiety is to joke about it. By making light of a situation, we can often reduce the tensions and carry on more effectively than we might have done otherwise. In addition, talking over our problems and anxieties with someone else can be helpful, as can quietly thinking the problem through by ourselves. Sometimes people cry about a problem and this enables them to let off steam and to feel better, at least for a while. Others forget their anxiety temporarily by sleeping, daydreaming, gorging themselves with food, getting physical exercise, masturbating, drowning their anxieties in alcohol, alleviating some of the pressure by taking drugs, or deliberately thinking about something other than the anxiety-producing situation. It can also help if one avoids those situations that are likely to make a person feel anxious. The young man who feels apprehensive whenever he asks a girl for a date, for example, can avoid this anxiety by no dating (although his solitary life may produce a different kind of anxiety). Within recent years tranquilizers and other kinds of medications have become useful chemical techniques for lowering anxiety. Then, especially among Christians, prayer and the comforts of Scripture are helpful and widely used. Finally, it should be recognized that some people handle anxiety by telling everyone about their problems and insecurities. This does not always do much to reduce the anxiety, but since it can bring sympathy and special treatment from others, the anxiety is more tolerable.

These different ways of coping with anxiety are sometimes used deliberately and at other times are brought about by unconscious influences. While all can lessen our feelings of anxiety, it does not necessarily follow that they are all equally desirable or effective. Furthermore, 'some of these can be used to help us avoid facing the real causes of our anxieties. The person who drinks excessively, for example, may find that this helps to dull the feelings of anxiety but this is done so effectively that the cause of the anxiety may never be dealt with. People who joke a lot, refuse to think about their problems, or spend a lot of time daydreaming might also be dealing with symptoms of anxiety but never really get to the underlying cause. Even prayer and perpetual reading of the Scriptures can be ways to avoid facing up to and dealing with a problem that might be readily solvable. Think again of the young man who is anxious whenever he asks a girl for a date. To read the Scriptures and pray about his anxiety might help with his feelings, but it would also help if he could put some action behind his prayers and simply learn how to call girls to ask for a date. Whenever possible, it is best to face up to our anxieties and the situations which produce anxiety, and then try to do something about these problems. The normal person tries to do this, when necessary with the help of a counselor, but other people (neurotics) remain in a highly anxious state. They refuse to bear the pain of facing their anxiety, and they live in tension, always trying to hide their feelings and to keep from being overwhelmed by the anxiety that continues to stir them up.

The Christian and Anxiety

What about the Christian who feels high anxiety and has a great tendency to worry? How does all of this apply to the believer or nonbeliever who is anxious about his finances, dangers of living in his community, bad influences on his children, problems with his marriage, sin in his life? How do Christians react when psychology says that a little anxiety is a helpful thing, but the Bible says, "Have no anxiety about anything"?[9]

We should realize that the older versions of the Bible, including the King James Version, do not use the word "anxiety." More often the word "fear" is used meaning much the same thing. Where the more modern translations use "anxiety," it appears that the word is used in two ways: as fret and worry, and as healthy concern.

Anxiety as fret and worry is always condemned. In His Sermon on the Mount, Jesus instructed His followers to "not be anxious (worry) about your life, what you shall eat or what you shall drink, nor about your body, what you shall put on. ... Do not be anxious about tomorrow," that is, worry about the future.[10] Paul instructed the Philippians that they should "have no anxiety about anything,"[11] a phrase which Kenneth Wuest, the Greek scholar, has rendered, "Stop perpetually worrying about even one thing."[12]

Anxiety in the form of fret and worry comes because of a sinful turning from God. Instead of acknowledging His sovereignty and preeminence we have shifted the burdens of life onto ourselves and assumed that we alone can handle the problems that we face. When man turns from God and becomes his own god, increased anxiety is inevitable. Perhaps it is not surprising, then, that in an age of increased godlessness there is also increased anxiety.

Happily, however, the Bible tells us what to do about this fret and worry. We must bring our anxieties to Christ,[13] confessing our alienation from Him and our self-centered attempts to handle our own problems. We must put Christ first in our lives[14] and cast our anxieties on the one who cares for us.[15] Notice that this action is followed by peace, rest, and freedom from anxiety. "Have no anxiety about anything," Paul wrote, "but in everything by prayer and supplication with thanksgiving let your requests be made known unto God. And the peace of God, which passes all understanding, will keep your hearts and minds in Christ Jesus."[16] In the midst of a world of pressure and anxiety, therefore, the God of the universe gives peace and comfort.

All of this is not meant to imply that God becomes simply a tranquilizer, an opiate, or an escape hatch that frees us from all concern and lets us go through life with a "couldn't care less" attitude. The Scriptures teach quite the opposite! While anxiety in the form of fret and worry is wrong and should be yielded to Christ, *anxiety in the form of realistic concern* is healthy. In the same letter to the Philippians in which Paul said to "have no anxiety," he also spoke approvingly of Timothy's being "genuinely anxious" for the welfare of the church at Philippi.[17] Elsewhere, Paul admitted that he himself felt a great deal of anxiety[18] but the word translated "anxiety" in these passages does not imply fret and worry. Instead, it connotes "caring for" or "showing a real concern for."[19]

Paul could honestly write that he wasn't anxious (that is, plagued with worry) about the possibility of being beaten, cold, hungry, in danger, or otherwise persecuted. But he was anxious (that is, concerned) about the churches and the welfare of other believers. Likewise, people today cannot be both committed to Christ and paralyzed by worry and fretful anxiety. But neither do they go through life with a complete lack of concern for the world around them. "The end intention of the gospel," wrote one Christian psychologist, "is to release man *from* the egocentricities of anxieties of life and. . .to release man *to* a concern for the welfare of others."[20] We must realize and acknowledge the power of God and must cast our cares upon Him.. But at the same time we must keep a realistic, healthy, genuine and active concern for the issues of life, including the welfare of others.

What does all of this say about life today? Psychology and the Bible both agree that there is nothing wrong with being concerned about the problems of life. Indeed, this is really very healthy, especially when the concern is focused upon the needs and welfare of others. But the Bible and psychology also agree that to take a blasé attitude or to be immobilized by excessive worry are also unhealthy. When this happens, we should be willing to honestly look at why we feel as we do, seeking, when necessary, the help of a Christian friend or counselor. In all of this we must trust in Christ to help us with the problem of anxiety as He has promised.

Questions for Further Thought and Discussion

1. What is anxiety?
2. How do you feel when you are anxious?
3. Suppose a church member feels anxious about speaking at a meeting of the congregation. Is such anxiety good or is it bad? Is it normal or abnormal?
4. What causes anxiety in people in general?
5. What causes anxiety in you?
6. Ponder the ways in which people cope with anxiety. Do some of these seem healthier than others? Do you think an over-reliance on one or two of these would be bad?
7. Which of the above methods for coping with anxiety do you use most often?
8. In II Corinthians 11:28 (RSV), Paul comments about a "daily pressure" on him because of "my

anxiety for all the churches." How do you explain this in view of Philippians 4:6 (RSV)?

9. Should a Christian ever be anxious? If so, when should he be anxious? If not, why are we anxious so often?
10. How can you meet the anxiety in your life?

Footnotes

1. Levitt, E. E. *The Psychology of Anxiety*. Indianapolis: Bobbs-Merrill, 1967, pp. vii, 1.
2. Marmor, J. Anxiety. In *The Encyclopedia of Mental Health* Vol. I, New York: Franklin Watts, Inc., 1963, p. 216.
3. Many of the research studies are described in Levitt, op. cit.
4. The study is reported in Janis, I. L. *Stress and Frustration*. New York: Harcourt, Brace, Jovanovich, Inc., 1971.
5. Meehl, P., et al. *What, Then Is Man?* St. Louis: Concordia, 1958, p. 123.
6. Levitt, op. cit., p. vii.
7. Ibid., p. 192.
8. In panic situations, however, anxiety often becomes so great that we stop thinking rationally and become irrational in our actions.
9. Philippians 4:6, RSV.
10. Matthew 6:25, 34 RSV.
11. Philippians 4:6, RSV.
12. Wuest, K. S. *Philippians in the Greek New Testament for the English Reader*. Grand Rapids: Eerdmans, 1942, p. 110.
13. Matthew 11:28.
14. Matthew 6:33.
15. I Peter 5:7.
16. Philippians 4:6-7, RSV.
17. Philippians 2:20, RSV.
18. II Corinthians 11:28, RSV.
19. Wuest, op. cit., pp. 80, 81.
20. Oates, W. E. *Anxiety in Christian Experience*. Waco, Texas: Word, 1971, p. 155.

CHAPTER 2

Discouragement

When I was a young child, there was a little song we used to sing in Sunday school. The words were neither complicated nor difficult to remember:

> I'm so happy.
> I'm so happy.
> I'm so happy, happy, happy,
> happy, happy, happy,
> I'm so happy.
> I'm so happy.
> 'Cause Jesus is a friend of mine.

When people, such as the teachers in my Sunday school, believe that the God of the universe is a friend, there is certainly cause for rejoicing. But is it normal or even desirable for individuals to be bubbling over all the time with effervescent happiness? The little song implied that perpetual jubilation should characterize Christian men and women, that we should never get discouraged;

but the fact is that we all do. Each of us experiences discouragement at times. Some people find that depression and despair become a way of life.

Discouragement is as old as man himself. If we look into the Bible, for example, we discover that there were many times in the ancient past when people showed discouragement. The Old Testament records one situation when the children of Israel became "much discouraged" in the midst of their wilderness wanderings.[1] The people had been in the wilderness for a long time and probably were tired. Miriam, Moses' sister, had died recently and the people had experienced a long drought. They were clearly in a complaining mood as they arrived at the borders of the country called Edom. Edom was shaped somewhat like the letter "U" and to get past this country the children of Israel had two alternatives. They could either go directly across the country from one side to the other or they could walk a long detour around. It probably didn't take them long to decide that they should ask the King of Edom for permission to cut across his land. But quickly and in no uncertain terms the King said "no," and when the children of Israel asked again, giving assurances that they would not pollute the land in any way, the King of Edom came out with a mighty army and made it very clear what would happen if the Israelites dared to step one foot onto Edomite territory. Faced with the prospect of going the long way around Edom, the Israelites became even more discouraged.

Many years later, in another part of the Middle East, we see a scene of discouragement which the Bible records in the book of John.[2] A man named Lazarus had died and Jesus announced to His disciples that He wanted to go to the place where Lazarus had been buried. The disciples did not understand this at all. Why, they wondered, had Jesus waited until after the death of Lazarus in order to make the trip and why was He going on a journey that was extremely dangerous? The attitude of the disciples was expressed by Thomas. "Let's all go along with Him," Thomas said. "We might as well all die together."

When the little band arrived at Bethany where Lazarus had lived, the family members were grieving, the professional mourners were wailing, and the friends and relatives were trying to bring comfort to the bereaved. As if this wasn't enough, there were religious leaders standing nearby making critical comments because Jesus had taken so long to get there and had not prevented Lazarus from dying. So discouraging and unhappy was the whole scene that Jesus was deeply moved and wept himself.

When we move to the Twentieth Century, we see that there are many people in the world—including committed Christians—who are very unhappy and discouraged. In the United States alone it is conservatively estimated that about 200,000 people attempt suicide every year, and of these 25,000 are successful. This means that on the average somebody tries to kill himself every three minutes and once every 21 minutes somebody succeeds. Most of these people are discouraged, depressed, and deeply unhappy with life. In addition, there are millions of people who have never contemplated or tried suicide but who periodically get discouraged. So common is the problem, we could say that the person who never gets discouraged is highly unusual and in many respects abnormal.

The Causes of Discouragement

People can get discouraged for a number of reasons. One of the most common of these is *frustration over our inability to accomplish some task*. When a person gets frustrated because he can't succeed at doing something, he often gets discouraged at the same time. Sometimes this frustration and discouragement come because the task is too long or too time-consuming. This must have caused part of the discouragement in the children of Israel since they had a long, hard journey ahead of them and were frustrated to learn that the trip could not be shortened.

In a modern situation, students today frequently get discouraged when they are a long way from completing their course of study. Educators often refer to this as the "sophomore slump." When the student arrives at college, he comes with an enthusiasm which often continues through the first year, but when the novelty and excitement wear off and the student comes back for his second year of study, he recognizes that the road ahead is very long. This causes him to get frustrated and discouraged. Perhaps it is not surprising that among students, suicide is now the second largest cause of death.

People also get frustrated and then discouraged when a task is too difficult. Have you ever seen a young boy building a model airplane? These used to come in a box with what seemed to me like millions of parts. I never completed the formidable task of putting one of these planes together because I used to get frustrated over the difficulty of trying to get all of the pieces together correctly. Invariably I would get discouraged and quit. All I could see was the seemingly insurmountable difficulty of the task.

Closely related to this is the frustration and discouragement which comes because a project just doesn't seem to be succeeding. Perhaps we don't have a long task and the work may not even be difficult but even so there are times when we never seem to accomplish what we want. Moses, Joshua, Elijah, Job and David all got discouraged because things didn't go the way they had hoped. Jeremiah preached his heart out but nobody responded (except with occasional laughter) and he became a very discouraged "weeping prophet." People today get discouraged when they aren't successful in molding children, winning a contest or an election as they had hoped, getting a job or an award of some kind, or being given a good grade on a test. Sometimes we even set up goals that we cannot possibly reach and then feel discouraged because of our lack of anticipated success.

The second major cause of discouragement is *the behavior of others*. The Scriptures instruct fathers not to provoke their children lest these little ones become discouraged.[3] The word "provoke" means to irritate or to be too exacting and sometimes we get discouraged because people provoke us. They put impossibly high demands on us (or at least we think their demands are too high) or they are highly critical of something we have done or failed to do. Because of these actions or criticisms from others, we get discouraged.

A third major cause of discouragement is *separation from people we love and respect*. This unhappiness can come either when we are separated permanently, as with death, or temporarily. Everyone knows the sadness and discouragement that are usually present when a loved one has died, but sometimes this begins even prior to death. Terminally ill patients and their families, for example, get discouraged not only because of the frustration of a long disease but also because of their dread of the coming separation.[4] "I won't be with them anymore," the patient thinks, and his relatives prepare for a new kind of life without the loved one. Some of the same kind of discouragement occurs when there is divorce or the breaking of an engagement. In addition, there can be sadness when the separation is temporary. Little children, who have no real time sense, show despair and discouragement when they are hospitalized.[5] Older people are sad and feel a sense of loss when their children go away to school, when a couple goes to the mission field, or whenever there is some other kind of temporary separation. Even some sickness is a form of discouragement, a grief reaction brought on by separation.

Some writers have suggested that a *lack of purpose in life* can also cause discouragement. Philosophers talk about existential despair. By this they mean a deep discouragement which comes because men have no direction and no apparent meaning in life. This lack of purpose may help to explain the discouragement of drifting college students, of housewives whose lives seem to consist primarily of doing dishes and changing diapers, of people in their 40's and 50's who are disappointed because they have not accomplished more in life but who see little hope for change, or for retired people who feel unwanted and no longer useful.

In addition to these psychological causes of discouragement we must recognize that sometimes the cause is primarily *physical*. Women who have recently had a baby or who are going through the menopause sometimes are prone to get discouraged usually because of hormone imbalance. People of both sexes know that when we are tired, hungry, "out of shape," or not feeling well, we have a lowered ability to resist discouragement.

All of this does not hide the fact, however, that the causes of discouragement are often *spiritual*. In writing to the Corinthian church, the Apostle Paul indicated that he had had a period of discouragement and he seemed to blame this on the devices of Satan.[6] To get people depressed must surely be a tactic of the Devil who wants to see people, especially Christian people, ineffective, unproductive, and hindered in their work.[7] There is also the possibility, however, that some of our discouragement comes from God. He too may hinder our earthly ambitions, and this could lead to discouragement, especially when we fail to grasp the wisdom of God's divine plan for our lives.

Characteristics of Discouragement

How do discouraged people act? Most obvious are feelings of sadness, unhappiness, frustration and disappointment. There may be tears and crying, accompanied sometimes by worry, anxiety about the future, or a desire to be alone and unbothered by others. Sometimes the person feels guilty and angry with himself, especially if he has reason to believe that the discouraging situation was brought on by his own actions.

Three other typical marks of discouragement were shown by the nation of Israel when they were refused passage through Edom. First, the people were highly critical and complaining. This still happens in discouraged persons who often find fault and criticize strangers, their fellow workers, their neighbors, other Christians, their families and sometimes even God. Secondly, the Israelites felt self-pity—the tendency of discouraged people to bemoan their fate and wallow in their problems. Then there is apathy which leads to slowing down and perhaps stopping our normal activities. The children of Israel decided to quit and die in the wilderness.

Today many suicidal persons apparently make the same decision. Even people whose discouragement is mild lose the motivation and enthusiasm to keep pushing on with their activities. Sometimes these people get careless in their grooming. They may stop eating. And they don't bother to spend time in prayer or Bible study.

These symptoms and the discouragement which they reflect are very common. Almost everyone gets discouraged at times, and in mild form we show many of the above characteristics. Most of us, however, can rise above our troubles sooner or later and keep going, but there are some who can't quite snap out of it that easily. These people sink into deep despair, sometimes even when the problem is relatively minor or when there are hopeful signs of improvement. Such deeply depressed people are perpetually unhappy, withdrawn socially, inactive, and plagued with feelings of hopelessness, helplessness, and deep despondency. Often there is intense anxiety, concern over physical aches and pains, and a tendency to blame one's self for the trials of life. This intense type of discouragement is beyond the scope of this book. It is usually dealt with by a competent psychiatrist, psychologist, or other mental health professional. Frequently the severely depressed person is counseled intensively, and often he is given anti-depressant drugs or shock treatment.

Dealing With Discouragement

There are at least six healthy ways to deal with discouragement.

First, we can recognize and accept the fact that all of us get discouraged at times. This is part of being human.

Once I taught a class in experimental psychology. My students were required to work with pigeons and rats. We taught these little animals complicated learning tasks and, although we never did this in our laboratory, we read about psychological studies in which animals were given mild electric shock and their responses recorded. Now in all of these projects, the animal didn't really know what was going on (at least we assumed he didn't). There was no way for us to tell him what we were doing as experimenters or why we were doing it. Even if one of my students could have taken the role of a pigeon or rat and communicated the details of our experiments, the animals still would not have been able to comprehend because their brains were too small.

It seems that this situation is similar to the way in which God looks down on us. He, who controls the universe and causes or permits discouraging situations to arise, knows what He is doing and why. But we cannot comprehend God's plan with our small brains and from our limited perspective. Remember Job? God and Satan talked together about Job's troubles,[8] but, according to the Bible, Job never knew why he experienced his problems.

Still, in His mercy God has given us some hints of why discouragement and other problems come into our lives. Sometimes difficulties are to bring glory to God. This is why Lazarus was allowed to die.[9] Sometimes the problems bring spiritual growth, greater patience, and more humility on the part of the sufferer or people who knew him.[10] At times God chastises us as an expression of His love.[11] More often, however, we simply cannot understand why God acts the way He does or why problems enter our lives. Instead we must accept the difficult conclusion that a discouraging situation is with us for reasons we cannot understand.[12]

A second healthy reaction to discouragement is trust—a renewed dependence on God.[13] Like Job, in the midst of his trials and discouragements, we must learn to say, "Though He slay me, yet will I trust in Him."[14] This isn't very easy. Many people trust that God can save us eternally, but they do not trust He will be with us on earth, even though He has promised to do so.[15] In the wilderness God sent poisonous snakes, and the Israelites looked on the brass serpent which Moses put on a pole in response to God's commandment. These discouraged people trusted God for deliverance, and it was only then that they started moving again.[16]

This brings us to a third healthy reaction to discouragement—meaningful activity. My wife and I once visited a lady who had been recently widowed. We arrived to find her digging around some roses. "I'm not much interested in flowers anymore," she said, laying down her trowel and taking off her gloves, "but my husband would have wanted me to keep busy and really this is the best thing for me." As this woman knew, the discouraged person should remain active, should resist the temptation to sit around in despair and self-pity. Activity just for the sake of doing something is fine, but it is much better if we can take some action which will help us to overcome the problem. The best kind of activity is that which is directed towards improving our undesirable situation and making things different.

Fourth, to overcome discouragement we need to keep perspective. When we experience an emotion like discouragement it is often easy to look for the bad in the situation and never to see the good. There is a tendency to conclude that all is hopeless, to expect the worst, and to do nothing about improving our circumstances. Here is one place where a concerned Christian friend can help as the discouraged person talks over the problem, expresses his feelings, gets a more realistic evaluation of the situation, and considers some practical ways of improvement. At times, for example, it may be necessary to lower our high aspirations or to overlook the criticisms of those people who have put us under pressure. At other times we may have to change our behavior in some way or attempt to see the situation as others see it.

Closely related to this is a fifth suggestion— trying to uncover the causes of the discouragement. Sigmund Freud believed that insight into the causes of our problems was the first (and often the only) step in solving problems. Certainly it isn't always easy to understand the causes of one's feeling. Sometimes we need a friend or counselor to help us see the source of our unhappiness.

Finally, we need to be alert to our physical condition. Plenty of sleep, periodic exercise, and a balanced diet can all help us meet existing discouragements and be less overwhelmed by problems in the future.

Implications for Christians

There is nothing wrong with singing, "I'm so happy . . . 'cause Jesus is a friend of mine." This *is* a cause for happiness but we must never get the idea that it is unchristian or unspiritual for people to be unhappy at times. Periodic discouragement is a part of life, and although believers can always be glad for their relationship with Christ and for their awareness of His sovereignty, there is nothing in the Bible to imply that we should always be grinning with happiness and bubbling over with exuberance. On the contrary, there are times when a Christian should weep.

Dr. John R. W. Stott, rector of All Souls Church in London, once made a systematic study of the Bible and identified several times when weeping is appropriate.[17] Stott has distinguished between "tears of nature and tears of grace."

The first of these, tears of nature, comes because we are human. These are tears that flow in response to the trials of life, when we are parting, when we are grieving, or when others are having problems.[18] In such situations the Christian can be aware of God's presence and God's control but he might also weep. We do not sorrow like those who have no hope[19] but there is nothing wrong in sadness and crying. Jesus wept at a funeral. Indeed, it is quite natural and part of our humanity.

The second type of tears, the tears of grace, are shed because we are believers. These tears are rare among Christians today but were present in Bible times. This includes tears over our own sin[20] and weeping over the lost condition or sin of others. Jesus shed such tears when He wept over Jerusalem.[21]

Dr. Stott concludes his perceptive article with these words:

> The fundamental error underlying our modern tearlessness is a misunderstanding of God's plan of salvation, a false assumption that his saving word is finished, that its benefits may be enjoyed completely, and that there is no need for any more sickness, suffering, or sin, which are the causes of sorrow.

> This is just not true. . . . The fruits of this salvation have not yet been fully garnered. And they will not be, and cannot be, until the end comes when Christ returns in power and glory. The ravages of the Fall have not yet been eradicated either in the world or in Christian people. We still have a fallen world, full of sorrow because full of suffering and sin. . . .

> . . .The eyes that do not weep are blind eyes—eyes closed to the facts of sin and of suffering in ourselves and in the rest of humanity. . . .[22]

A time is coming when there will be no more crying, suffering or despair; until then, however, let us recognize that problems and discouragement will be part of our lives even when we are committed Christians. Let us realize that the Holy Spirit will comfort and guide in times of discouragement, and then let us rejoice—in the midst of our life on earth—as we recognize the sovereignty of God, His guidance in the present, and His promises for the future.[23]

Questions for Further Thought and Discussion

1. Why, in general, do people get discouraged?
2. What causes *you* to get discouraged?
3. Make a list of the characteristics of discouragement as presented in the chapter.
4. Do you or your friends show any or all of these characteristics in times of discouragement? Are there additional characteristics which you show?
5. Do you agree with the following words from a well-known hymn?

    > Have we trials and temptations?
    > Is there trouble anywhere?
    > We should never be discouraged,
    > Take it to the Lord in prayer.

6. In this chapter the author suggests that discouraging situations come from Satan *and* may come from God. Do you agree or disagree? Can you find Scripture to support your opinion?
7. Does Psalm 42:5 present a realistic way of meeting discouragement? Is this the best way to meet the problem? Is it the only way? How would you answer the criticism that to "hope in God" is really just

wishful thinking and a very ineffective way of meeting the problem?

8. What are some other ways for dealing with discouragement?

9. How do you meet discouragement in your life?

Footnotes

1. Numbers 20:14-21.
2. Chapter 11:1-44.
3. Colossians 3:21.
4. Kubler-Ross, E. *On Death and Dying.* New York: Macmillan, 1969.
5. Janes, I. L., et. al. *Personality: Dynamics, Development and Assessment.* New York: Harcourt, Brace & World, 1969, pp. 172-174.
6. II Corinthians 2:11.
7. I Thessalonians 2:18.
8. Job 1:1-12; 2:1-6.
9. John 11:4.
10. John 11:15, I Peter 1:6-7.
11. Hebrews 12:6.
12. Romans 11:33
13. Psalm 42:5.
14. Job 13:15.
15. Jude 24; II Thessalonians 3:3, Matthew 28:20.
16. Numbers 21:6-10.
17. Stott, J. R. W. "When Should a Christian Weep?" *Christianity Today.* Vol. 14, November 7, 1969, pp. 3-5.
18. I Peter 1:6; II Timothy 1:4; Acts 20:37; John 11:35; Romans 12:15.
19. I Thessalonians 4:13.
20. Exra 10:1; Psalm 119:136; Philippians 3:18.
21. Luke 19:14.
22. Stott, op. cit., p. 5.
23. For a Christian approach to discouragement, see the book by D. Martyn Lloyd-Jones, *Spiritual Depression: Its Causes and Cure.* Grand Rapids: Eerdmans, 1965.

CHAPTER 3

Anger

Several decades ago a child psychologist began a careful study of the emotional behavior of infants and very young children.[1] Careful observation led the psychologist to conclude that anger is one of our earliest emotions. As adults, all of us get angry at times. Some are more prone to this than others and many find it extremely difficult to control our tempers even after we reach adulthood.

The Meaning of Anger

As a common experience, anger needs no definition. It should be pointed out, however, that anger involves at least two characteristics. First, anger is an emotional reaction which is felt and in some way expressed. When we get angry, we usually feel hindered, threatened and aggressive. Little children throw tantrums and express their anger by kicking, crying, screaming, thrashing about, and pounding their little fists. In adults tantrums usually disappear, but angry feelings may be shown in facial expression, tone of voice, choice of words, and sometimes in physical violence. Even when we learn to remain outwardly cool, calm and collected in times of anger, the muscles still tense, pulse increases, breathing gets deeper and sugar content increases in the blood.

But anger is more than experience of emotion. It is also a motivator, something which spurs us on to attack, flee from, or rise above a situation. When we speak of anger, therefore, we speak of an emotion that is felt and a motivating force that drives us to some kind of action.

The Causes of Anger

Why do people get angry? Most of us could draw on personal experience to answer that question, but it is probable that our answers could fit into one of several categories. First might be the view that anger is inborn, some kind of tendency we all possess, perhaps from the time of conception. This view has been most clearly expressed by those who have studied aggression. Freud, for example, held that man is aggressive by nature and that his anger and hostilities are sometimes even directed inward against himself. More recently, a German psychologist named Konrad Lorenz wrote a popular book in which he suggested that all animals, including man, are dominated by an aggressive instinct.[2]

Still, there reamins little to support the view

that aggression and anger are inborn.[3] Anger may be universal and we cannot deny that it is often a reflection or outgrowth of man's sinful nature, but to say that anger is inborn is to go beyond both scientific and Biblical evidence. (In spite of this some people will go on believing that anger is innate because such a view can give a good excuse for continuing with angry outbursts. When one believes that anger is an inborn trait, the conclusion often follows that nothing can be done about it, that there is no use in trying to change, that there is no other alternative.)

But I hasten to add that some people, by nature, are more inclined to explode in anger than others. Because people apparently differ in their inherited temperaments, it is probable that some have a greater tendency to "blow their top" than others. But although we may inherit different potentials for becoming angry, the actual experience and expression of anger is brought about by other causes.

A second view, and one which seems to have more scientific support, is that anger is brought about by learning. We all know that some people express their anger more openly than do others. Some of us have a tendency to explode in outward rage while others seethe inside but outwardly "keep their cool." These individual differences are more than variations of expression, however. They apparently reflect differences in the actual *experience* of anger. One psychologist has expressed it this way: "Although anger and hostility are normal ... we differ greatly both

individually and as groups in the degree and the
frequency of the hostile feelings we experience."[4] These differences stem in large extent
from one's learning or past experience. Anthro-
pologists' findings support this. In her studies of
South Sea islanders, for example, Dr. Margaret
Mead found some tribes trained their children to
be aggressive and angry, while other groups
trained their children to be peaceful and non-
aggressive.

It appears that in our society we teach people
to be angry and aggressive. When he was arrested
several years ago, H. Rap Brown, the militant
Black leader, described violence and outward
expression of anger as something "as American
as apple pie." And Arthur Schlesinger, Jr., the
noted historian, has written that violence is "the
American way."[5] We settled the American West
by violence, he suggests, we settle international
disputes by violence, and we solve most television problems by violence. Parents who indis-
criminately permit their children to watch TV
cartoons often fail to recognize that seeing television violence can stimulate the viewer to vio-
lent behavior himself.[6]

A third cause of anger has been suggested by
researchers at Yale University who developed a
theory that anger and aggression always occur in
response to frustration. A frustration is an obstacle (an event, physical barrier, or some person)
which hinders our progress towards a goal
(Figure 3-1). A flat tire in the midst of rushing
to church, a sickness that comes as we embark
on a vacation, a telephone that rings while we

Figure 3-1.

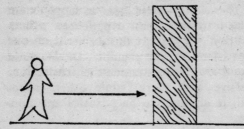

GOAL

The Meaning of Frustration. Frustration arises when our progress toward some desired goal is blocked.

try to finish a project or get a bath—these are all frustrations; they all block our progress towards some goal.

How much people feel frustrated depends on the importance of the goal and the size of the obstacle. To have no lemonade in the refrigerator when we want a cool drink is less frustrating than to have, say, no room for us in the college we want to attend. The man in the slums has greater, more lasting frustrations and a greater desire to get out of his undesirable living situation than does the man in the comfortable suburb. The ghetto dweller therefore is more likely to be frustrated and hence more inclined to be angry and aggressive.

In their famous book[7] the Yale researchers proposed what has come to be known as the "Frustration-Aggression Hypothesis." Briefly stated, this says that when people are frustrated they always become aggressive.

In trying to understand the causes of anger, all three of the above suggestions might have some validity. While it is possible that some people are innately more prone to be angry than others and that anger depends to some extent on our learning and past experience, we can also state that anger often arises as a result of frustration.

Reactions to Anger

What do we do when we get angry? Very often we simply deny that we are angry and pretend we are not. Christians are especially prone to this approach because we have been led to believe that anger is bad, that it is wrong to express or even feel this emotion. Let us emphasize again, therefore, that all of us experience anger at times and that this anger will be expressed either in ways which are healthy and appropriate or in ways which are unhealthy, destructive and inappropriate.

Another way people respond to anger is to overcome or remove the source of the frustration. If a person, object or situation is making us angry, this means we try to deal directly with the underlying cause of the trouble. We may attack the source of our anger verbally—as when we tell someone off—or nonverbally in the form of a clenched fist or Molotov cocktail. Sometimes, anger may be actively handled in the form of an open attack or it can be much more passive and subtle, directed toward another person in the form of critical comments, cruel jokes, or unkind actions.

More effective is the approach that tries to overcome the obstacle more constructively. We may try, for example, to understand and communicate with the person making us angry or perhaps work to remove the obstacle in our environment that prevents us from attaining our goal. At other times, we may reset our sights a little lower and work to achieve something more easily attained. These approaches to anger, all of which deal with the problem at its source, are illustrated in arrow No. 1 of Figure 3-2.

Figure 3-2.

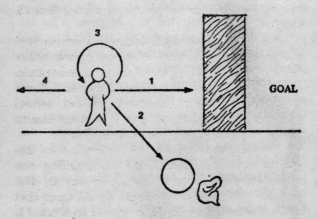

Reactions to Frustration. When faced with frustration an individual may (1) attempt to deal directly with the source of the frustration, (2) direct his anger onto another object or person, (3) turn on himself or (4) withdraw from the frustrating situation.

Arrow No. 2 represents a second way we can deal with anger. This involves attacking not the source of our anger but something or someone else. Psychology books call this *displacement*. When frustrated by the boss, instead of attacking him we may criticize our wife or children. Some form of displacement occurs whenever we see a person slam a door in anger or pound his fist on a table; he is attacking an innocent piece of wood that bears the brunt of his anger. This is an explanation for much prejudice. We may be angry about an issue but we direct our anger toward an innocent group of people unable or unlikely to strike back. It is easier to blame Jews or Negroes or Catholics or liberals for our problems instead of facing up to our own inadequacies or our own inabilities to overcome frustration.[8]

Probably much of the violence in our society is a learned reaction wherein we attack either the source of our frustration or a substitute. Throwing the dean out of his office is a direct attack when we are frustrated about school policy. It is an indirect attack if we eject him to protest the military-industrial complex.

Attacking a substitute can often be an unhealthy and inefficient way of handling our anger but sometimes it is a good way to deal with the problem. Most people would agree that to hit a little golf ball when we are frustrated is much healthier than to hit our employer.

A third reaction to anger may seem more surprising. Sometimes we turn against ourselves. This is illustrated in the third arrow of Figure

3-2. A turning upon oneself is usually unconscious, and may take the form of self-criticism,
the development of physical ailments, increased
feelings of inferiority, and sometimes self-
destruction. Suicide victims, for example, are
often angry with themselves. So possibly are
many people who are accident prone. (Some
writers have concluded that accident prone persons are unconsciously attempting to hurt themselves because they feel guilty or because of
anger with themselves.) Sometimes an attack
upon oneself can also be a subtle way of attacking others, since by showing how much one
hurts and is suffering, one can make others feel
sympathetic and guilty.

Turning upon oneself can be bad, but not
always. Sometimes anger at ourselves motivates
us to work harder. Because of this we can often
avoid more failure, frustration and anger-
producing situations.

A fourth reaction is withdrawal—to forget
about the situation, to give up, to think about
something else, or to find satisfaction elsewhere.
Withdrawal can be physical (when a person
leaves the room) or psychological (when he stays
but withdraws in his thinking). The person who
counts to ten before exploding in anger is really
withdrawing psychologically and temporarily,
giving himself a few seconds to gain composure.
Of course, some of us never withdraw and as a
result get into situations which should be left
alone, since they just aren't worth getting angry
about. But those who refuse to withdraw for a
few moments to gain perspective expand un-

important things into issues of great significance. Someone may beat us away from a stop light, for example, and instead of forgetting it, we race to catch up. An inconsiderate clerk in a store may say an unkind word, but instead of letting her remark pass and withdrawing from the situation we start to argue. Many disagreements that become major issues in families, businesses or churches are not really worth arguing about.

However, while withdrawal can be a good way to avoid unnecessary conflict, there are times when it can be unhealthy. Sometimes to withdraw from a strong feeling of anger is really to push the anger out of conscious awareness and to deny it exists. But such repressed anger rarely fades away—instead it builds up inside and often leads to increased physical tension or to psychological disorders. If this anger remains repressed it can build up and eventually lead to irrational and uncontrollable aggression or retaliation. When this happens, often the person condemns himself in turn for his wicked feelings of hostility; this self-condemnation then makes him feel inadequate and his self-esteem fades.

When anger is present, therefore, we must first recognize that it exists and then attempt to control it. The word "control" can have two meanings. Sometimes to control means to eliminate, as when we talk about controlling forest fires. Anger which is destructive, completely self-centered, or leading to acts which are disobedient to God should be eliminated. At other times the word "control" means to guide, as when we control the wheel of a car. Sometimes feelings can be fully expressed but remain under control. When anger helps to remove injustice, to improve conditions, to eliminate sin, to reduce tension, or to bring about better communication, it is useful. Feelings should be expressed, providing we do not lose control.

Implications for Christians

According to Scripture, anger is unacceptable when it is hasty,[9] without real cause,[10] or long lasting.[11] We are instructed not to show vengeance[12] nor are we to keep company with furious and perpetually angry people.[13]

But anger is not totally condemned by the Bible. Frequently we read of God's wrath. We are told that Jesus got angry[14] (and when we think of Him with a whip driving moneychangers out of the temple it is hard to believe it did not involve feelings of anger). In Ephesians 4 we read that Christians are supposed to be angry, or to put it in the words of one Christian writer, there are times when we should "be good—and mad."[15]

The confusion over when a Christian can be angry is reduced considerably when we recognize that there are several Greek words that have been translated "anger" in the English New Testament.[16] The first of these is the Greek word *orge*, meaning intense anger that comes as a reaction against sin and wrongdoing. This is righteous indignation over sinful behavior and is the word used to describe the anger of Jesus in Mark

3:5. The same word is also used in Ephesians 4:26 when we are instructed to "be angry."

Some of us would say that a little anger is all right but a lot of anger is always wrong. Notice, that *orge* anger is, by definition, intense. When He drove the moneychangers out of the temple, Jesus showed *orge*. In Him, of course, this did not lead to sin but there is a danger it can do so in the rest of us. Because of this the Apostle Paul says, "Be ye angry (intensely indignant over sinful behavior) but be careful that you do not sin." Our *orge* must be strong but it must also be controlled.

The second Greek word is *parogismis*, meaning a bitter irritation and exasperation. It is the word that has been translated "wrath" at the end of Ephesians 4:26. This bitter anger is wrong and we should not let it persist in us.

The third Greek word, *thumos*, is used in verse 31 of Ephesians 4 where it has been translated "wrath." It refers to a boiling agitation or an outburst of intense feeling, and this, too, is wrong.

How do we get rid of *parogismis* and *thumos*? How are we as Christians to avoid exploding in uncontrollable outbursts of rage? The Scriptures indicate that we are capable of deliberate action: each of us should not let the sun go down on our anger. Each person should give no opportunity for the Devil to influence his anger. Each should put away anger.[17] This implies that we are all responsible for self-control. For some this may be more difficult than others but all of us are to work at controlling our anger.

Even when the Christian is instructed to do something, however, he has assurance of divine help. The Holy Spirit can give us power to replace anger and hostility with love, peace, patience, and self-control.[18] He can help us to honestly face our anger, to acknowledge its presence, to talk about it with some other person, to confess it to God, to express it in a healthy way and to control our anger so that it is constructive—bringing improvement to the situations around us—rather than destructive. With divine help we can learn to control the anger which periodically wells up in each of us.

Questions for Further Thought and Discussion

1. Is anger experienced by everyone?
2. What sorts of things make people angry?
3. What especially angers *you*? What is there about *you* that angers others?
4. How do people react to anger? Do all people handle anger in the same way?
5. How do *you* react? How do the people with whom you live react?
6. Is anger good or bad?
7. Is it wrong to get angry with another church member when he disagrees with your position at a church business meeting?
8. Is it ever right for a Christian to blow up in anger?. When Jesus got angry in Mark 3:5, did He blow up?
9. Suppose that a married couple has a disagreement at 10 p.m. They are both tired and angry. What should they do to handle their anger? Does Ephesians 4:26b mean that they should stay up until the anger disappears?

Footnotes

1. Bridges, K. M. B. Emotional Development in Early Infancy. *Child Development*, Vol. 3, 1932, pp. 324-341.

2. Lorenz, K. *On Aggression.* New York: Harcourt, Brace & World, 1966.
3. Montagu, M. F. A. (ed.) *Man and Aggression.* New York: Oxford University Press, 1968.
4. Coleman, J. C. *Psychology and Effective Behavior.* Scott, Foresman, 1969, p. 409.
5. Schlesinger, A., Jr. *Violence: America in the Sixties.* New York: Signet Books, 1968.
6. Berkowitz, L. (ed.) *Roots of Aggression: A Re-Examination of the Frustration-Aggression Hypothesis.* New York: Atherton Press, 1969.
7. Dollard, Jr., and others. *Frustration and Aggression.* New Haven, Conn.: Yale University Press, 1939.
8. Buss, A. H. *The Psychology of Aggression.* New York: Wiley, 1961.
9. Proverbs 14:17; 16:32; Titus 11:7; James 1:9.
10. Matthew 5:22.
11. Ecclesiastes 7:9.
12. Proverbs 19:11.
13. Proverbs 22:24
14. Mark 3:5.
15. Hope, N. V. "How to be Good and Mad," *Christianity Today.* Vol. 12, July 19, 1968, pp. 3-5.
16. The three Greek words are discussed in the exposition of Ephesians 4 which appears in Wuest, K.S., *Word Studies: Ephesians and Colossians.* Grand Rapids: Eerdmans, 1953. See especially pp. 113-114.
17. Ephesians 4:26, 27, 31.
18. Galatians 5:19-23.

CHAPTER 4

Guilt

As part of my training to become a psychologist I spent several months working in a clinic for physically handicapped children. Each morning a number of parents would come to this clinic with their disabled children and the family would participate in two days of intensive diagnostic examinations. A pediatrician, orthopedic surgeon, child psychiatrist, physical therapist, social worker, and clinical psychologist would, at different times, meet with the parents and the child and then come together as a professional team to pool our knowledge and to discuss how the young patient could be helped.

One morning a mother came into my office and gave her appraisal of why she had a mentally and physically handicapped daughter.

"It is punishment from God," the lady stated.

"I was a missionary in Africa but when I came home on my first furlough, I met a man, fell in love, and got married. My husband is a fine Christian and he is good to me as well, but he never felt called to the mission field. Because I never went back, God has punished me with this sick child."

The woman who sat across the desk was obviously plagued with guilt. Her whole life was characterized by feelings of remorse because she had not remained a missionary.

Guilt has been described as the place where psychology and religion meet.[1] Probably there is no other topic which is of equal interest to both theologians and psychologists. Dr. Ernest Jones, a psychoanalyst who wrote a three-volume biography of Freud, once described guilt as the most difficult and the most important problem in the whole realm of psychology. Almost all of man's troubles, Jones believed, can be traced to our inner feeling of guilt.[2] All of the emotions discussed in this book, various types of mental illness, and many forms of physical sickness have, at times, all been thought to arise because people feel guilty. It may be, therefore, that guilt is the key concept around which this whole book should center.

The Meaning and Prevalence of Guilt

Guilt arises when we have consciously done something wrong—when we have violated ethical, legal, moral, or religious standards. Often, but not always, guilt is accompanied by feelings of regret and self-condemnation. Sometimes guilt arises because we have done something wrong and wish we hadn't, while at other times we feel guilt because we failed to do something we knew to be right. The Episcopal prayer book states it concisely in the prayer of confession: "We have done those things which we ought not to have done and we have left undone those things which we ought to have done and there is no health in us."

Most of us fail in the way of that prayer every day. We say an unkind word, we procrastinate, we get too busy to spend time with our families, we fail to meet an obligation, we have some immoral thought, or we ignore our conscience and deliberately sin. All of this brings guilt often accompanied by feelings of remorse and self-criticism.

But even if we have no reason to feel guilty in ourselves, other people have a way of stirring it up within us. It is a very useful way to manipulate other people, to get our children (or our parents) to do what we want. The teenager who complains, "Everyone else is doing it. . ." often wishes his parents to feel guilty because of their stubborn resistance. Such parents sometimes yield in order to relieve their "guilt." The husband who bellows to his wife, "I drink because you nag all the time," pushes the blame onto her and tries to make her feel guilty, thus relieving himself of responsibility for his own actions. The pastor who threatens to resign because people don't go along with his programs or come to his services may be manipulating them to feel sorry for him, to feel guilty, and, therefore, inclined to change their behavior. Children attempt this too. Recently our four year old wanted some candy and was distressed when her mother said no. "If you don't give it to me," my daughter pouted, "I'll be very unhappy and I'll cry." This attempt to make her mother feel guilty and give in was not successful, but I wondered where she had learned that making others feel guilty is a good way to manipulate them into doing what you want. (I would like to think she learned the tactic from neighborhood children, but I have a suspicion she may have learned it from me!)

Types of Guilt

Guilt is so widespread in our society, so common an experience, and so often mentioned in theological and psychological literature, that several types have been identified. These can be divided into two categories: objective guilt and subjective guilt. Objective guilt exists apart from our feelings. Here the person has broken some legal standard, and he is guilty whether he feels it or not. Subjective guilt is a feeling or inner experience of remorse because of one's actions.

Objective guilt is further divided into three types. First, social guilt. Here the individual is guilty because he has broken a law or accepted rule that most people around him accept. I drive 80 in a 30-miles-per-hour zone and I break the law. I may or may not feel guilty, but if I happen to pass a policeman I will probably be stopped and given a fine or court summons. But sometimes social guilt comes because we have broken an unwritten law. If I engage in an act that, according to those around me, wrongs another person or group of people, I am guilty of harming a relationship with others. I may criticize someone unkindly, ignore my children, pass by a person in need, or gossip maliciously. In doing these things I may have broken no legal written laws, and I may not even feel bad, but I have violated the social expectations of my society. Thus, I am guilty of engaging in an act that puts a barrier between other people and myself.

The second type of objective guilt might be called psychological guilt. This arises because I have done something which goes against my own personal standards. The Apostle Paul discussed this in Romans 14 and I Corinthians 10. There was nothing legally wrong with eating meat that had been offered to idols and for most people there was nothing morally wrong with it. For some, however, this was a sinful act; to consume that meat would have produced guilt in the eater because he had ignored his inner standards and conscience. In a more modern setting, the student who decides that he should read four books every month may experience guilt if he does not meet this goal. Psychological guilt in this student comes only because he has not reached his own very personal and private goal.

A third type of objective guilt arises from our relationship with God. Sometimes called ontological or theological guilt, it refers to our standing before God. According to the Bible, all men have sinned and have come short of the glory of God.[3] We have all disobeyed God, ignored His voice at times, and selfishly refused to trust Him. We are all guilty of breaking our relationship with God, even though we might not feel such guilt.

Most of us would feel uncomfortable if we had broken social law (social guilt), violated our conscience (psychological guilt), or deliberately ignored God (ontological guilt). However, it is possible to do all of these things and not feel even a twinge of guilt. The hardened criminal may murder and not feel anything. Millions of people, including Christians, forget God every day and thus sin against Him. While these people *are* guilty before God they *feel* no sense of guilt because of their actions. The matter of feelings brings us to the second broad category of guilt, *subjective guilt*.

When we talk about guilt, most of us refer to the subjective feeling that people so often experience when they do wrong or have unacceptable (to them) thoughts and wishes. The person who cheats on his income tax, the Christian who misses a church service, or the wife who thinks unkind thoughts about her in-laws, all may feel a great sense of self-blame and humiliation.

These subjective feelings of guilt may be appropriate or inappropriate. Appropriate guilt feelings arise when we have broken a law and feel remorse in proportion to the seriousness of our action. Inappropriate guilt feelings are those which appear to be out of proportion to the seriousness of our action. Some people, for example, feel nothing even when they act in a way which seriously violates the law, goes against their own moral standards, and is a sin against God. This lack of guilt feeling is inappropriate, highly unusual and might even be classified as neurotic. At the opposite extreme are those people who are overwhelmed by feelings of guilt. They feel guilt very strongly even when they have done something which others consider to be minor.

I once counseled a lady who for many years had taken care of an elderly and demanding father-in-law. One day, in the midst of anger, the lady told her father-in-law, "Shut up!" For days afterward this woman worried, chided herself and felt condemned because she had spoken so harshly to an old man. Also, at times those who express constant guilt feelings are playing a game with themselves, saying they feel guilty about one thing when really it is something else that is bothering them. They may, for example, feel great remorse about missing a church service but whether they recognize it or not, they really are guilty of something else—ignoring God in their lives.

Causes of Guilt

How does guilt arise? In the first place guilt comes about because our conscience bothers us. Most psychologists think of the conscience as an inner experience of right and wrong that develops as we grow up. By listening to the teachings of our parents or teachers and by watching others, we learn what they say is right or wrong; good or bad, moral or immoral. Soon the standards of others become our standards. They become part of ourselves, and thus when our actions are at odds with these standards, we feel uncomfortable and guilty.

Although psychologists all agree that the conscience is acquired, scriptural evidence suggests that standards of right and wrong may also be inborn.[4] God apparently has written some standards within the hearts of men; when we violate these standards, we are guilty.

This brings us to a second reason for feeling guilt: supernatural influences. We know that the Holy Spirit convicts men of their sin, speaks to us about what is true and right, and reminds us of the teachings of Jesus.[5] Unlike other religions Christianity gives us a perfect person, Jesus Christ, who is a standard by which we mold our lives. When we ignore or fall short of this standard, the Holy Spirit reminds us of it.

But the Holy Spirit is not the only supernatural influence that may bring about feelings of guilt. Satan also accuses us.[6] He also arouses guilt feelings and makes us feel uncomfortable, especially if we are obedient to God. Therefore, while guilt feelings are sometimes healthy and beneficial (when they are aroused by the Holy Spirit), at other times they are unhealthy and harmful (when they are aroused by satanic forces). How do we tell the difference? God's standard of right and wrong is clearly outlined in the Bible, and we can be sure that the Holy Spirit never directs us to do something contrary to the written Word of God.[7]

The Consequences of Guilt

When we think of guilt most of us probably think of something undesirable. While this is often true, we should realize that guilt and guilt feelings can also be desirable. If we never became aware of ontological guilt, for example, we might never see the need for a Savior. If we never had any guilt feelings, we might be more inclined to act in ways which would harm other people and harm ourselves. Guilt and guilt feelings, therefore, are not always bad. Sometimes they are constructive and helpful.

Still, guilt feelings often influence us adversely—especially when we rationalize guilt and pretend it does not exist. We do this when we make up excuses to explain our guilt away: "Of course I cheated on my income tax!" we say to ourselves, "but everybody does it." Or, "Certainly I went over the speed limit but there weren't any other cars around and they probably expect most people to do a little over the posted speed anyhow." Equally common is the tendency to pass the buck by blaming someone else for our guilt-producing behavior. Adam blamed Eve who in turn blamed the serpent. Hitler blamed the Jews for his difficulties and at the end of his life wrote, "It is true that neither I, nor anybody else in Germany, wanted war in 1939. It was wanted and provoked exclusively by those international politicians who either came of Jewish stock or worked for Jewish interests. After all my efforts toward disarmament, posterity cannot place the responsibility for this war on me."⁸ This also happens when we blame our friends for their bad influences or we deny we are responsible for our actions since so much behavior is determined by our past experiences, or the influences of our parents. (More and more people, it seems, are claiming they cannot be held responsible for their actions since they are the helpless victims of unhealthy childhood experiences.)

When we push guilt from our conscious awareness, we can be sure it will come back to haunt us in other ways. Denied guilt, for example, often causes physical illness. The mere energy of keeping the guilt out of one's mind can put a strain on the body and cause it to break down. It is also quite possible that guilty people punish themselves unconsciously by getting sick. This may sound ridiculous until you recognize that according to several estimates, between 50 and 75 percent of all patients who go to a medical doctor are suffering from physical illnesses that are emotionally caused.⁹ If we are physically sick, we get a lot of sympathy and almost nobody holds us responsible for our actions—including the actions that are causing the guilt.

Denied guilt can also cause depression. Here the person has done something for which he feels guilty but instead of facing his guilt he develops feelings of hopelessness, worthlessness, despair, and discouragement.¹⁰

A third way denied guilt influences us is by causing self-destructive behavior. I once counseled with a very bright young man who had never succeeded in anything. As we talked it became apparent to me that he really didn't want to succeed. He was unconsciously sabotaging his own success in order to pay for some guilt he was trying to keep hidden. Perhaps you have heard of the religious men in the Philippines who, on Good Friday of each year, walk through the streets beating themselves with whips, literally tearing their backs to shreds. Here self-inflicted pain comes because the individual feels guilty and thinks he should punish himself. And, as mentioned in the previous chapter, some writers have even suggested that accident proneness may characterize people who are unconsciously angry with themselves for past deeds.[11]

Fourthly, denied guilt can cause neuroses. Often the guilty person develops what psychologists call an obsessive-compulsive neurosis in which the individual feels a compulsion to do something over and over again since such repetitious acts seem to help one to fight off guilt. Lady MacBeth's repetitious handwashing is a good example from Shakespeare. This neurosis also characterizes the behavior of many religious people. When a person feels he must rigidly attend every church service, serve on every committee and engage in every ritual, these may be unconscious attempts to ward off guilt feelings. For these people life becomes a great burden. Their religion becomes a list of do's and don'ts; they never know the real joy that comes from a guilt-free, Christ-centered life.

Dealing with Guilt

For many years psychiatrists and psychologists have struggled with the problem of how people can be freed from guilt. One of the most common solutions has been to change our view of what is right or wrong. "Lower your standards," some psychologists say, "and learn to do as you please without feeling guilty." Such a solution has been widely accepted in our culture, but since it only deals with guilt feelings (not objective guilt), it rarely works. Men today feel increasingly confused, discouraged, anxious, and guilty in spite of the lowering of moral standards. Guilt has to be handled in some other way.

Our whole legal system in this world is built on the assumption that the one who breaks the law must pay; all of the burdensome symptoms we have listed on guilt are really attempts by men to pay for their guilty behavior. The Bible, however, tells us that Christ has already paid. [12] It is because of Jesus Christ's death for our wrongdoing that we are able to deal with our guilt permanently and effectively. To do so there are five basic and necessary steps.

The first of these is *repentance*. In the preceeding pages we have avoided using the word "sin." The Bible is clear, however, in stating that men are sinners and that it is sin which causes guilt and guilt feelings. To be free of guilt, we must recognize, as did the Psalmist King David, that whenever we do wrong we are really sinning.

against God who alone is sinless.[13] To overcome our guilt we must recognize that apart from God, no man can really do good and that our so-called righteous acts are really as acceptable to God as a pile of filthy rags.[14] In short, we must be sincerely ashamed and sorry that we have sinned against a holy God.

But there is more to removing guilt than feeling sorry for what we are and have done. Some people spend their lives in self-debasement and still feel guilty. The second step in dealing with guilt, therefore, is *confession*. The Scriptures show us two kinds. First, there is confession of our sins to God. This step is necessary if we ever hope to experience forgiveness.[15] This confession of specific sins should be a daily occurrence if we expect to be free from guilt and guilt feelings. In addition, the Scriptures also teach the importance of confession to other men. The writer of the book of James encouraged this and so did Jesus when he instructed men to be reconciled to each other.[16] Recently, a psychologist at the University of Illinois has made this the central feature of his system of counseling. Don't confess to everyone, this psychologist says, but tell your sins to the person or persons whom you have wronged and ask for their forgiveness.[17]

This brings us to the third step in dealing with guilt, *forgiveness*. When we confess, God forgives. This is a simple truth with profound implications for guilty man. But notice that we are not only to receive forgiveness, but we are to forgive others when they confess to us. The Lord's Prayer mentions this, and in Matthew 18:21-35 we read of an occasion where Jesus discussed the issue at length. Some of us confess sin to God (and are forgiven by God) but don't feel forgiven. Might it be that our refusal to forgive others stands in the way of experiencing the relief that otherwise would come?

It is also important that we forgive ourselves. Many of us are forgiven by God but go on feeling guilty because we have not forgiven ourselves. Perhaps these people don't really believe that God has forgiven or that He is able to forgive. Like the father who once brought his ailing son to Jesus, these people must honestly cry, "Lord, I believe; help thou mine unbelief."[18]

The fourth step in dealing with guilt is summarized in the word *restitution*. In the Bible we read about a man named Zacchaeus who, besides being a tax collector, was also a crook. One day Jesus met him and forgave him for his dishonesty. After Zacchaeus accepted the gift of forgiveness, he decided to pay back everything that he had stolen with interest. This paying back was not necessary in order for Zacchaeus to be forgiven but it grew out of his changed life.[19]

According to the Bible, there is no need for men to pay or make restitution for their sins. In fact, we are not able to do this, which is why Christ paid instead. But when we realize that our sins are paid for and forgiven, it is natural that we should respond by giving to others and by making restitution as an act of worship and thanksgiving.

The final step in dealing with guilt is *changed behavior*. Like the woman taken in adultery, we must go our way and sin no more.[20] We must yield ourselves to the living Christ and commit ourselves to His service. We must count on Him for courage and strength to overcome guilt and to resist the temptations of the Devil. We must realize that even if we sin again, God has made provision to remove the guilt.[21]

To accept all of this is difficult. We have human bodies that are subject to temptation and we know that too often we yield.

Sometimes we find that we are worrying and berating ourselves about minor sins while we ignore something major. Sometimes we sincerely want to rid ourselves of guilt but find that we have difficulty following the five steps that are outlined above. At such times we can often find help if we share our concerns and evaluate our guilt by talking with another person.

When we sin, there is little value in engaging in morbid introspection, in making excuses for our sins, or in hiding our guilt. Instead, we can confess our sin knowing that it will be forgiven and that the guilt will be removed because Christ died not for our sins only, "but also for the sins of the whole world."[22]

Questions for Further Thought and Discussion

1. What is the difference between objective guilt, subjective guilt and guilt feelings?

2. Why do people feel guilty?

3. What sort of things make *you* feel guilty?

4. Do you agree with the author's suggestion that guilt feelings may arise both from the influence of the Holy Spirit and from the actions of Satan?

5. Are guilt feelings always bad?

6. How does guilt cause depression or neurosis?

7. Why would a psychiatrist such as Dr. Ernest Jones call guilt the most difficult and most important problem in psychiatry?

8. What is a good way to handle guilt?

9. In what practical ways can you deal with guilt in *your* own life?

Footnotes

1. This is the subtitle of a book by Belgum, D. *Guilt: Where Religion and Psychology Meet.* Minneapolis: Augsburg, 1970.

2. Reported by Busby, D. "Guilt," *Journal of the American Scientific Affliation,* Vol. 14, 1962, p. 113.

3. Romans 3:23.

4. Romans 2:14-15.

5. John 16:8, 13; 14:26.

6. Job 1:9-11; Revelation 12:10.

7. I John 4.

8. Reported in Knight, J. A. *Conscience and Guilt.* New York: Appleton-Century-Crofts, 1969, pg. 119.

9. Belgum, op. cit., p. 49.

10. Mowrer, O. H. *The Crisis in Psychiatry and Religion.* Princeton, N. J.: Van Nostrand, 1961, p. 97.

11. Belgum, op. cit., p. 50.

12. I Peter 3:18.

13. Psalm 51:4.

14. Romans 3:10; Isaiah 64:6.

15. I John 1:9.

16. James 5:16; Matthew 5:24.

17. Mowrer, O. H. *The New Group Therapy.* Princeton, N. J.: Van Nostrand, 1964.

18. Mark 9:23-25.

19. Luke 19:1-10.

20. John 8:11.

21. I John 2:1, 2.

22. Ibid.

CHAPTER 5

Inferiority

Have you ever looked into the windows of a hospital nursery and wondered what it must be like to be a little child? Have you ever watched two and three year olds scampering into church or playing in a park and wondered what life for them must be like? All of us have had the experience of being young children, of course, but our memories of those early days are very vague.

Shortly after the turn of the century a famous psychiatrist in Austria named Alfred Adler attempted to analyze the thinking of very young children.[1] He recognized that babies and toddlers are really very helpless little creatures who are constantly reminded that they are smaller, less capable, less skilled, less successful, and less powerful than almost anyone else around. As a result, all children develop what Adler called feelings of inferiority. These feelings are not all bad since they motivate the child to overcome his deficiencies or inadequacies.

As Adler thought further about this and counseled with his patients, he reached another conclusion. Little children, he decided, are not the only people who feel inferior; all of us feel inferior to some extent. To "be a human being," he once wrote, "means the possession of a feeling of inferiority that is constantly spurring us on to greater achievements."[2] Feelings of inferiority and incompleteness are not abnormal. They are the great driving force of mankind, the real motivation in life.

But what if the feelings of inferiority are too strong? What if instead of motivating us to better things, these feelings cause unhappiness, discouragement, frustration, a sense of inadequacy, or feelings of worthlessness? What if it is true, as one writer has claimed,[3] that 95 percent of the people in our society have lives that are characterized by mild feelings of inferiority, while millions of other find that inferiority feelings seriously interfere with their success and happiness?[4]

Cause of Inferiority Feelings

Psychologists and psychiatrists have had a field day in trying to discover why so many people feel inferior. In the beginning of our discussion we must recognize that some of us feel inferior because in many respects we *are* inferior. When it comes to throwing a football, I am greatly inferior to Joe Namath. When it comes to preparing a salad, broiling a steak, or baking a cake, I know that I am inferior to my wife.

These inferiorities, and many like them, do not bother me because I am not much concerned about my poor athletic skills or my lack of expertise in cooking. Most of us recognize we have many inferiorities that bother us very little, if at all.

But what if there is an area in which we want to do well and can't? What about the teenager who wants to get on the school basketball team, but isn't good enough? What about the college senior who wants to go to medical school, but whose grades are too low? What about the career girl who wants to get married but fears that she is not attractive enough? These people often have strong feelings of inferiority because they are not successful in an area where they want very much to succeed. I once counseled with a man in his early twenties whose life history had been characterized by numerous failures. Everything he did seemed to turn out wrong; he had come to feel very inferior and inadequate. And, as a matter of fact, there were many indications that he felt inferior because he really was.

Other people feel inferior because they *think they are* inferior, even though they might not be. Most of us have met individuals who are really very capable (perhaps even outstanding) in their accomplishments, but who don't believe it. We may know people who by all indications have great potential but who don't think they can succeed.

There are several reasons why these capable people get the idea that they are inferior and inadequate. In the first place, many come to

think of themselves as being inferior because
they have been belittled by others. If parents,
teachers or spouses repeat enough times that a
person is no good, stupid, and unlikely to
amount to anything, it is not long until he
believes it. Soon such people belittle themselves
and act according to their beliefs.

At the opposite extreme are those people who
think they are inferior because they have been
pushed beyond their capacities by well-meaning
but insensitive parents or other adults. When
standards are set unrealistically high, failure and
feelings of inferiority become inevitable. Some
parents perpetually demand more than a child
can produce and eventually the youngster concludes, "I can never satisfy them," so he gives up
in frustration. I once knew a young lady whose
father was a perfectionist. According to this
father, his daughter's accomplishments were
never good enough. As a result, the girl always
felt inadequate, having learned from her father
to set standards for herself she was never able to
reach. It is hardly surprising that the girl had
great feelings of inferiority.

Closely related to this is a third reason why
people think they are inferior: frequent failure.
Some very capable people who have understanding and encouraging parents, who are not pushed
beyond their capabilities, still have inferiority
problems. Why? Because of various circumstances these people experience such frequent
failure they convince themselves they are no
good. The person who fails because of frequent
illness or "bad breaks" is an example.

Sin in our lives is a fourth reason for thinking we are inferior and a very common cause of inferiority in Christians. When a person sins, or engages in some action which goes against his conscience, there are often feelings of guilt, self-condemnation, and inferiority. Forgetting the loving and merciful Savior who forgives and forgets about our sins, this person remains in his guilt. He concludes that he is a worthless person and that something is wrong with his spiritual life because he is continually tempted and so often yields.

How we feel about ourselves can also be influenced by group membership. I once taught at an inner-city university situated on the outskirts of a ghetto. Many of my students were black. They felt that they were often treated as second-class citizens and as members of a group which other people considered to be inferior. Here were students who felt inferior because they belonged to a group which society treated as inferior. If you live in a culture where black is not beautiful and you happen to be black, where Jews are considered dishonest and you are Jewish, or where Fundamentalists are thought to be bull-headed and narrow-minded and you are a Fundamentalist, then you may feel inferior because of your membership in a group which is downgraded by others.

Over-protection can also cause people to feel inferior. By dominating, smothering and fluttering over children, parents sometimes prevent their offspring from making any mistakes. Children therefore are ill-prepared for life and when

they reach adulthood they experience many failures and accompanying feelings of inferiority.

Of course, many people rise above the adverse
circumstances of life and feel no inferiority in
spite of their being belittled, pushed, unsuccessful, sinful, part of a rejected group or over-
protected. It all depends on how we react to
circumstances and how we handle our failures.
For some, failure is a spur to greater effort and
success, but for many others these problems of
life lead to increased feelings of inadequacy and
inferiority.

To this point we have assumed inferiority
feelings are something unpleasant, but it seems
some people actually enjoy feeling inferior. Certainly there are benefits to be gained from convincing ourselves and others that we are inadequate in some way. When we claim to be
inferior, other people can feel sorry for us,
giving us extra privileges and extra attention.
And the person who belittles himself has another advantage: he never has to face the pain of
attempting something and discovering that he
really is a failure.

I can see a lake where water skiers are active
on summer weekends. Periodically some visitor
asks me if I ever ski on the lake. Quite frankly I
think this would be great fun but I never have
learned how to water ski. Since I cannot swim, I
feel somewhat insecure about going into the
middle of a lake where all I have to keep me
afloat are two little boards and a life jacket.
Now as long as I tell people that I just can't
water ski, I can use that as an excuse to stay out

of the water. I never have to confess that I am really afraid of drowning or making a fool of myself as I try to stay on top of the water. In my own mind I could (if I wanted to) build up great fantasies about my water skiing potential. I could daydream about skimming across Diamond Lake to the acclaim of all who watch, but I will never have to risk drowning or facing the fact that my fantasies might be unrealistic because I have a wonderful excuse for staying on the shore: I don't know how to water ski. By belittling my skiing abilities and claiming to be inferior I am able to get myself off the hook. A more common example are students who frequently belittle themselves in front of teachers or classmates. "I just can't do math," a young girl might complain. This gets sympathy from her parents (and sometimes from a teacher or classmates) and it becomes an acceptable excuse to avoid taking a math course; it also provides a convenient justification in case the student does in fact do poorly in the course.

The problem with convincing others that we are inferior is that before long we end up convincing ourselves. If we try to persuade other people that we cannot do mathematics, before long we believe this ourselves and we actually do poorly in the course, even though we may have high ability and high scores in mathematical aptitude tests (see Figure 5-1).

And if we succeed in convincing ourselves that we are inferior in order to be consistent with our own convictions, we act in an inferior way. Notice in the diagram that once we put in

Figure 5-1.

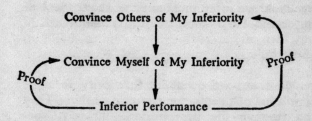

The Vicious Circle of Inferiority. The person who tries to convince others of his inferiority eventually convinces himself. Then, in order to be consistent with his beliefs he acts in an inferior way. This, in turn, proves to the individual and others that he really is inferior.

an inferior performance, this comes back as proof to ourselves and to others that we are indeed inferior. This is called a vicious circle. A person can get on to the cycle at any point and when he moves in the direction of the arrows, his feelings of inferiority increase and his performance gets worse.

Before leaving this we should note that we rarely belittle everything about ourselves. Instead the tendency is to downgrade ourselves in the areas we most want to succeed. In the words of one psychiatrist, "The capacities that are belittled are usually the ones in which the individual desires most ardently to excel. . . . This connection is so usual that one may guess from the focus of the self-belittling tendency where the greatest ambitions lie,"[5] The person who makes an issue of his intellectual inferiority often wants to succeed in that very area. The musician who makes an issue of his musical inferiority or the housewife who complains about her inability to cook are often most anxious about succeeding in those areas most frequently mentioned.

Alternatives to Inferiority Feelings

What can we do about inferiority feelings? For a lot of people the answer is nothing. They go through life brow-beaten, unhappy, convinced of their worthlessness and frustrated because they feel so inferior.

For others, inferiority feelings are attacked but in self-defeating and unhealthy ways. Many times we do this unconsciously, without realizing what we are doing. Some people, for example, hide their insecurities and never acknowledge that they feel inferior. Sometimes such people display a loud bombastic appearance of great self-confidence. To the world they look very self-assured but this is really a front which hides their insecurities and feelings of incompetence. For others, hidden feelings of inferiority come out in the form of physical problems like ulcers, asthma or migraine headaches. When this happens, the illness is often used as a convenient excuse for inactivity and continued feelings of inferiority. Another self-defeating attitude is to wallow in one's inferiorities and to talk about them whenever the opportunity arises. By their actions, and sometimes by their words, these people make a sympathy play. "Poor little me," they complain, "look how tough life is for me and how inferior I am." Such people almost take pride in their inferiorities and sometimes they develop a "my-inferiorities-are-better-than-your-inferiorities" attitude.[6] These are often the people who unconsciously set their goals so high that failure and continued feelings of inferiority are assured.

Another self-defeating reaction is to criticize and to knock down everyone else so that (in our own minds) we are the "top dog." This is what the Pharisees did in Jesus' day.[7] They criticized everybody and walked around in smug superiority. The person who is highly critical is also frequently insecure and concerned about his own inferiorities.

Hiding one's inferiorities, wallowing in them, or becoming highly critical of others may all seem like foolish ways for dealing with feelings of inferiority, but the people who adopt these techniques often are unwilling to change. They go through life always feeling inferior but persisting in those self-defeating activities which maintain the status quo and prevent the person from living a life more pleasant and satisfying.

Happily, however, people who feel so inferior as to be defeated need not go through life with those feelings. There are effective ways we can handle our inadequacies. To begin, it is important to recognize that people can feel inferior both in terms of their worth and in terms of their ability. These should not be confused. In terms of *worth* all men are equal. A person's race, wealth, sex, status and responsibilities have nothing to do with how he is seen by God. In God's sight all men are of equal worth. This does not imply, however, that all men have equal *ability*. Because of special capacities, intellectual endowment, experiences and past opportunities, people differ in their accomplishments and capabilities. In terms of abilities and gifts, therefore, all men are not created equal.

The Apostle Paul recognized this and wrote that people have different gifts and different responsibilities.[8] When he looked at himself, Paul admitted that he wasn't as intelligent as some other men, that he didn't speak in lofty words of wisdom, that he had a tendency to be nervous and that he was physically unattractive. But Paul also recognized that he was a good writer, that he was being used of God and that he was a faithful soldier of Jesus Christ.[9] You will note Paul didn't hide his weaknesses, he didn't wallow in them and he didn't boast of his strengths in an attempt to be superior to everyone else. And he didn't criticize or knock everyone else down. Instead he said, in essence, I am moving out to serve Jesus Christ in the best way that I can, recognizing that I have both strengths and weaknesses. A willingness to take a realistic self-appraisal, therefore, is the first step in dealing with our inferiorities.

The second healthy approach to this problem is somewhat similar: we can change our self-image. As we grow into adulthood, all people develop a number of opinions, attitudes and feelings about themselves. These opinions, which psychologists lump together and call self-opinions, self-concept or self-image, develop as a result of our experiences with other people and with objects. The baseball player may recognize that he is a good athlete because of his past experience in handling the ball and because of the acclaim given by the fans. If he is well liked by girls, but has difficulty in chemistry, he decides that he is a good athlete and a good date, but a poor student. These conclusions become part of his self-image. Since we all have different abilities, past experiences, and physical skills, we all differ in our self-concepts.

Behavior largely depends on our self-concept, or to say it more simply, how we act depends on what we think of ourselves and how we see ourselves. Scholarly books in psychology have emphasized the importance of a positive self-concept, of thinking highly of one's self and of developing a high amount of self-esteem.[10] This comes easily if we have had many experiences that convince us of our worth.

But what if we haven't had such experiences? Can we train ourselves to think positively? Norman Vincent Peale thought so and wrote a book entitled *The Power of Positive Thinking* that sold millions of copies.[11] Dale Carnegie thought so and influenced millions of people with two books that encouraged people to change their self-image so that they could *Win Friends and Influence People* and *Stop Worrying and Start Living*. More recently a plastic surgeon named Maxwell Maltz has produced a bestselling book entitled *Psycho-cybernetics*. It starts like this: "Discovery of the self-image represents a breakthrough in psychology." And its first chapter is entitled, "The Self Image: Your Key to a Better Life."[12]

Psychologists tend to be skeptical of self-help books like these, perhaps because we are jealous of their popularity. But even the stuffiest of psychological writers will recognize that self-image is important and can be changed. It is possible to think of yourself differently, and this in turn can influence your actions. A more positive self-image, therefore, works against feelings of inferiority.

A third healthy way in which we can overcome feelings of inferiority is to attack our feelings head-on and attempt to change our behavior. If we are number two, we can always try harder to be number one. Still, a competitive struggle to be the man at the top is not always desirable, nor is it satisfying. Probably most of us would agree with Adler that there is a better way to change our behavior, a more satisfying solution to the problem of inferiority. This does not come from competition with other men. It comes instead as a man strives with himself to outdo his own past performances. Everyone has heard of Winston Churchill's unimpressive career as a student, but Churchill overcame his scholastic difficulties and rose to become one of the greatest statesmen and writers in British history. On this side of the Atlantic, Franklin D. Roosevelt had polio but overcame this to become President. Earlier, Teddy Roosevelt, who had been a weakling in his youth, became a physically stalwart man. These men knew their strengths and weaknesses and they accepted them; but then they went on to develop their strengths and to overcome their weaknesses.

Attempting to improve on our own past behavior can, therefore, be an effective way of countering feelings of inferiority.

Implications for Christians

People who are followers of Christ are likely to feel a little uncomfortable about the suggestion that we should think of ourselves more positively, that we should strive to outdo ourselves, or that we should recognize our good characteristics and attempt to improve them. Somehow this seems unchristian and wrong for people who often sing of "... such a worm as I."

I once counseled with a fine young lady who felt that it was Christian to be inferior. She found numerous Bible verses to support the position that to be humble meant that a Christian should be inferior and a failure. This student made the assumption that humility and inferiority are the same thing, but they are not. Inferiority refers to a persistent dwelling on one's undesirable actions and characteristics, but humility implies that we can accept our strong and weak points and that we realize both our nothingness before God and the fact that God has given all of us certain gifts, abilities, and responsibilities. According to the Bible, all men are sinners; all are nothing when contrasted with the glory and greatness of God.[13] But God loves us. He recognizes that we are helpless and he sent his Son to die for us.[14] When an individual acknowledges his sinful status and asks God to control his life, Christ transforms that person. The believer becomes a new creature, a child of God, and a joint heir with Christ of God's blessings.[15] How can one feel inferior, then, when he is the object of God's love and concern, when he has been redeemed by the Son of God, and when he is given such attention by the Creator of the universe? The Christian shouldn't moan of his inferiority. On the contrary, he should rejoice because of his new position in Christ's family. It is true that we didn't deserve to be God's children. It is true that eternal life comes as a gift and not as a payment for our good works.[16] But it is also true that we have been elevated to a position of close friendship with the God of the universe. This is a reason for rejoicing!

Too often we forget that. We look at the world around us with its values and its scorn of Christianity and we assume that our religion really does attract inferior people. Before long we begin to think that we are inferior. We belittle ourselves and others, or we set impossible standards for ourselves, or we overprotect ourselves by withdrawing from the world into secure little cloisters. After a while we begin to feel safe and to enjoy our withdrawn state. We learn to love our self-centered worship, we enjoy wallowing in our assumed inferiorities, and we criticize others because they are not as spiritual or humble as we.

This kind of thinking needs to be changed. We must stop apologizing for our devotion to and dependence on a living God. It is time that we honestly acknowledged that while we are all sinners, we are valuable creatures because God created us, loves us and sent His Son to redeem us. If we have invited Christ into our lives, we are new creatures set apart to serve the living God. We don't all have the same gifts or abilities and we don't all have the same responsibilities. God doesn't call everyone to be a teacher or a deacon or a foreign missionary, but we do all have the same call to serve with whatever we have to give. According to the Bible every part of the body of Christ is necessary and important.[17] Periodically, therefore, we must pause to acknowledge these facts, to confess our inferiorities to Christ, and to commit our lives wholly to him. Then both our self-image and our behavior will change.

Do you feel inferior? To some extent this isn't bad. It may mean that you honestly recognize your weaknesses as well as your strengths. It may mean that you realize your place in God's universe. It could even spur you on to do better. But let's keep the Scriptures in perspective. Wallowing in our inferiorities, taking pride in having admitted them is sinful. It involves a failure to accept the fact that God has actually changed us and given us abilities that can be used for His service. The writer of the Book of James gives good advice: humble yourselves in the sight of the Lord, but then remember that "Christ shall lift you up."[18] Let us not take such pleasure in our inferiorities that we refuse to be lifted up, that we refuse to be used or that we refuse to think as God intended His people to **think.**

Questions for Further Thought and Discussion

1. Are feelings of inferiority good or bad?
2. What causes people to feel inferior?
3. What causes *you* to feel inferior?
4. Is a person who fails frequently doomed to life-long feelings of inferiority?
5. What are some self-defeating ways of dealing with inferiority feelings? What are some healthy ways?
6. How do you deal with feelings of inferiority in your life? Are there better ways of meeting the problem?
7. Is it acceptable for a Christian to develop the power of positive thinking?
8. It has been said that Christians are the world's most inferior people. Do you agree? Give reasons for your answer.
9. How can we help others to overcome feelings of inferiority?

Footnotes

1. See Adler, A. *Understanding Human Nature.* New York: Greenburg, 1927.
2. Mullahy, P. *Oedipus Myth and Complex: A Review of Psychoanalytic Theory.* New York: Grove Press, 1948, p. 116.
3. Maltz, M. *Psycho-cybernetics.* New York: Essandes Special Editions, 1968, p. 51.
4. Very often, we use the term "inferiority complex" to describe people who are seriously handicapped by their sense of inferiority. When this term was first suggested (by Alfred Adler, incidentally), it was used to describe something unconscious. The person with an inferiority complex really believed that he was inferior but he was not consciously aware of this self-evaluation. Psychologists still use the term inferiority complex in this way. When we are talking about a *conscious* concern over one's real or imagined inadequacies, it is more accurate to talk about "inferiority feelings."

5. Horney, K. *The Neurotic Personality of Our Time.* New York: Norton, 1937, p. 220.
6. See Berne, E. *Games People Play: The Psychology of Human Relationships.* New York: Grove Press, 1964, p. 84.
7. Matthew 23.
8. Romans 12:3-8; I Corinthians 12: Ephesians 4:11, 12.
9. I Corinthians 2:1-5; II Corinthians 10:10; II Timothy 4:7.
10. See, for example, Combs, A. and Snygg, D. *Individual Behavior* (rev. ed.). New York: Harper & Row, 1959.
11. New York: Prentice-Hall, 1952.
12. Maltz, M., op. cit.
13. Romans 3:23.
14. John 3:16.
15. II Corinthians 5:17; Romans 8:16, 17.
16. Ephesians 2:8, 9.
17. I Corinthians 12:14-28.
18. James 4:10.

CHAPTER 6

Pride

Professors are reluctant to admit it, but it is true nevertheless that most of what a student learns in school he quickly forgets. When I began college we were required to sit for three mornings a week in a class called Freshman English. The only thing that I can still remember from this experience is the name of the professor and a few lines from a poem by Shelley. According to the poem, there had once been an influential kingdom in a distant land ruled by a man named Ozymandias. This king was mighty, powerful, domineering, and so impressed with himself that he permitted a great statue to be erected in his honor. Over the centuries this statue had crumbled, and when Shelley described it, all that remained were two legs and a pedestal. The poet described the scene like this:

> . . .on the pedestal these words appear:
> "My name is Ozymandias, king of kings;
> Look on my works, ye Mighty, and despair!"
> Nothing beside remains. Round the decay

of that colossal wreck, boundless and bare
the lone and level sands stretch far away.

Historically, Ozymandias was an Egyptian phar-
oah who persecuted the people of Israel and
who, in righteous pride, called himself King of
Kings. Now he is remembered only by a poem
and a pile of crushed stones in a barren desert.

History is filled with examples of people who,
like Ozymandias, haughtily flaunted their greatness. Nebuchadnezzar, king of Babylon, boasted
of his power and majesty, but he went insane
before realizing that it was God—not a Babylon-
ian monarch—who was really King. More recently, Hitler thought of himself as the sovereign
ruler of a superior race, but Hitler's dreams and
empire collapsed in a mass of rubble.

We need not look at kings and dictators to see
examples of pride, however. Only recently after
I had given a talk on inferiority, a lady near the
back of the room stood up and confessed, "Inferiority isn't my problem. I am much more
concerned about pride. I am too impressed with
myself!"

She had a point. If you look into the Bible,
you will find that there are no warnings against
inferiority. Psychologists and psychiatrists coun-
sel every day with people who feel inferior;
millions of men and women are concerned about
their feelings of inadequacies, but the writers of
the divine Word of God never even mention the
subject. There are, however, numerous references to pride, especially in the book of Proverbs. Pride is sin, it is hated by God, and it

causes men to fall.[1] It is, in the opinion of one
contemporary preacher, "the mental and moral
condition that precedes almost all other sins.[2]

The Meaning of Pride

The word "pride" can be used in two ways.
Sometimes the word refers to "self-respect." I
am proud to be a Christian, we might say. I am
proud to be a follower of Jesus Christ, proud to
be a citizen of my country, proud to be a father
or a mother. Pride in the sense of self-respect
and self-esteem is not bad. As I tried to show in
the previous chapter, Christians should have this
kind of pride. Believers have good reason to
think well of themselves, not because we are so
good or worthy, but because of what God has
done for us in spite of our sinful nature. If
anyone wants to boast, the Bible says, let him go
ahead and boast but be sure that his boasting is
in what the Lord has done.[3] This is the basis for
self-esteem in the Christian.

When the term pride is used in the Bible,
however, it means something other than self-
respect. It usually refers to conceit, to self-
aggrandizement, to an arrogant superiority or to
an excessively high opinion of ourselves and our
importance. Billy Graham has called pride "that
revolting conceit which swaggers before men and
struts in the presence of the Almighty."[4]

This self-conceit can take many forms. Sometimes it involves open boasting and talking about
our achievements. At other times it may be seen
in an attitude of superiority as the Pharisees

displayed in the New Testament.[5] Usually, however, proud people are much more subtle. We drop bitter comments, for example, that make others feel inferior or guilty and this in turn enables us to subtly assert our superiority. "I read to my children for a least half an hour a day," a mother might mention, knowing full well that what this really says to her listeners is, "I am a better mother than you are. Don't you feel guilty and inferior because you don't do what I do?" Sometimes we express our pride by becoming overly critical of others. This, of course, implies to people around us that we are better since the criticisms which we apply to others rarely are applied to ourselves. In our churches we sometimes become like the hypothetical man who prayed:

> God, we thank thee that we are not as other churches: liberal, neo-orthodox, compromising, or even as some of the congregations in our denomination. We worship twice on Sunday, we attend midweek service, and some of us even tithe.
>
> We know that Thou art pleased with our militant stand for the faith once delivered, and we thank Thee that Thou hast enabled us to refuse courageously to have fellowship with those who do not dot their i's and cross their t's as we do. We earnestly pray, O Father, that Thou wilt convict these churches of the error of their ways and we pray that we may be an example to them. May they see us—separated, uncompromising, orthodox—and be filled with a longing to become like us.[6]

Sometimes we express our pride by withdrawing. Paul Tournier, the Swiss psychiatrist, describes this in one of his books.[7] He had become proud over his brilliant remarks in lectures, so he decided to stop making speeches altogether and to withdraw from the speaking circuit. Soon he realized that he was gloating over his "self-control" and ability to keep quiet. Periodically I am invited to speak at a church and this usually means I am expected to shake hands with the worshippers as they leave following the service. Early in my speaking career I decided that this boosted by pride and that it encouraged people to be hypocrites when they mumbled "wonderful message" on the way out. I decided, therefore, to avoid standing at the door, and as I gloated about this, it came to my attention that some people thought I was too snobbish to shake hands. As a result, I resumed my position at the door. Finally, we often assert our superiority by the strange tactic of telling everybody how inferior we are. "I'm such a terrible speaker," someone might say, and then he can gloat while he listens to people deny that this is so.

The Causes of Pride

There are at least five reasons why people develop pride. First, pride is very frequently seen in people who feel inferior. This may seem surprising, but pride and inferiority so often go together that some psychologists would say that they can never be separated.[8] The person who feels inferior tries to overcome his feeling by convincing himself and the world that he is really great. Thus, pride becomes a reaction against feelings of inferiority.

This is often seen in people who flaunt their achievements or boldly display their accomplishments and possessions. Often these are the people who feel the most inferior and insecure about what they have. I have noticed that young Ph.D.'s are sometimes very willing to display their academic accomplishments. They are much concerned about being called "Doctor," and they like to hang up all their diplomas to make sure that people are aware of their achievements. Later, when these people are more self-assured, such expressions of status are much less important and often no longer needed. In a different context, Billy Graham has observed that on state occasions the ambassadors and rulers of small nations are often resplendent in gold braid and glittering medals, while the leaders of great nations are dressed modestly.[9] Such a parading of ourselves covers the fear that we might not be as important as we would like to believe. By developing an ostentatious pride we are able to hide insecurity, anxiety, and fears that we might really be insignificant.

This parading of accomplishments has another outcome, however. While it may or may not impress others, it frequently impresses ourselves. "Look at my accomplishments," we say to ourselves, and along comes pride. Sometimes the proud person bullies his way through life. He likes to push others around, to get special privileges and to be waited on. If he doesn't get his way, he thinks nothing of humiliating others or taking revenge. By being insensitive to others he is trying to say, "I am important enough to do this." Frequently he convinces himself of his importance and sometimes such a person is able to convince others. But even as he develops proud delusions of his own importance, underneath he maintains that gnawing feeling that he might really be a nobody.

Secondly, we sometimes acquire pride through learning. In this highly competitive society, we are taught to develop the power of positive thinking about ourselves, to let others know of our accomplishments, to push ourselves ahead and to let no one push us around. In this struggle to get ahead, pride and the desire to succeed become a way of life everybody acquires. With all of this competition and struggle to push ahead, it is not surprising that some people who feel inferior learn to bluff.

Immaturity is another reason for pride. Little children are self-centered, stubborn, and mostly concerned with their own needs. As they grow older, most of them develop consideration for others, but this is not automatic. Some people never grow up. They remain dependent, irresponsible and self-centered. Freud called this condition *primary narcissism,* after a Greek named Narcissis who, according to legend, fell in love with his own reflection in a pool and pined away in self-admiration. Narcissism is not necessarily bad in young children; but in the adult it is bad. It is pride and a reflection of immaturity.

Fourthly, some people become proud because they are so lonely. Unconsciously, they flaunt themselves in attempt to be noticed and accepted, hoping that in the process they will establish contacts that they would not have otherwise.

A fifth reason for pride, and a cause from which all others probably stem, is sin. Although it is difficult to really know whether sin is a cause or a result of pride, the Scriptures are clear in their equating of sin and pride.[10]

The Cost of Pride

Erich Fromm, the famous psychoanalyst, has written that narcissism and pride affect men in four ways.[13] First, says Fromm, the proud person has an increased tendency to explode in anger.

> Normally a person does not become angry when something he has done or said is criticized, provided the criticism is fair and not made with hostile intent. The narcissistic (proud) person, on the other hand, reacts with intense anger when he is criticized. He tends to feel that the criticism is a hostile attack, since by the very nature of his ...(pride) he cannot imagine that it is justified.[14]

Because of his haughty manner, therefore, the proud person is prone to be discouraged. Other people are unlikely to accept his high self-appraisal so the proud person feels unappreciated, unwanted and unhappy. Sometimes this leads to the third reaction, psychological withdrawal. A proud person avoids the pain of criticism by ignoring it and the people who give it, pretending instead that the criticism does not exist. Then finally, the proud person tries harder

to convince others of his position and importance. This is the basis of much manipulation,
trying to force others to see us as we like to see
ourselves.

All of these actions cut the proud person off
from others. People dislike being with those who
subtly or blatantly display their pride. Such people make the rest of us feel uncomfortable and
we resent the implication that we are somehow
inferior. Proud people in turn often realize their
unpopularity and go through life pretending to
be humble but fail to give a very convincing
performance. Pride, by its very nature, cuts people off from each other.

But pride does something worse. It separates
us from God and leads to spiritual deadness. As
we have seen,[15] pride is sin, and sin is what
separates us from God. In Proverbs, chapter 6,
we read of seven things that God hates, and the
item which tops the list is pride.[16] Over and
over again this comes through the pages of Scripture. God resists the proud; He wants His people
to be humble.[17] Clearly, pride not only harms
us psychologically and separates us from other
people, but also alienates us from God and prevents spiritual growth.

Dealing with Pride

The answer to pride is not wallowing in our
inferiority. That really is unchristian, as we saw
in the previous chapter. The solution to the

problem of pride is very simple, although the cure takes a long time.

First, we must confess our pride. As we have seen, pride is sin and the first step to dealing with sin is always to confess it and to realize that God will forgive and cleanse us from all unrighteousness.[18] Then, having confessed, we must humble ourselves. There are several illustrations in the Bible of proud men who were humbled by God. Nebuchadnezzar was one, and so were Haman, Naaman, and Jonah. Whenever God humbled the person, however, the experience was very painful. The Scriptures do not say, therefore, that we should ask God to humble us. Instead we are told to humble ourselves.[19] To do this, we must change our words so that our talk is not boasting about ourselves. But we need to do more than talk differently. We must also develop different attitudes. In writing to the Romans, Paul warned every man "not to think of himself more highly than he ought to think; but to think soberly, according as God hath dealt to every man the measure of faith."[20]

This brings us back to where we were at the end of the previous chapter. We in ourselves are little, but God loves us and by sending His Son to die, He made it possible for us to be His children. We have been given the privilege of serving and knowing God personally. There is no need, then, for us to feel inferior, but neither is there cause to boast. Instead, our responsibility is to praise God, to enjoy Him, and to serve Him with the skills and responsibilities He has given to each of us. When we cast off the joint problems of inferiority and pride we have done much to conquer the stresses that make life difficult.

Questions for Further Thought and Discussion

1. What is pride?
2. Is pride good or bad?
3. Does the "prayer" in this chapter in any way describe you or your church?
4. Why do you think pride is so often mentioned in Scripture while inferiority is never mentioned?
5. Do you agree with the author's argument that proud people almost always are trying to hide their insecurities and inferiorities?
6. How can we deal with pride?
7. What does it mean to humble ourselves? How is it different from self-criticism and a perpetual talking about how terrible we are?
8. It has been said that the moment we tell people of our humility we lose it. "Humility is the one thing we can pray for but never thank God for." Do you agree with these statements?

Footnotes

1. Proverbs 21:4; 16:5,18.
2. Graham, B. *The Seven Deadly Sins*. Grand Rapids: Zondervan, 1955, p. 11.
3. Jeremiah 9:23-24; I Corinthians 1:31.
4. Graham, op. cit., p. 12.
5. Matthew 23.
6. Johnson, Roberta J. "Our Church's Prayer," *Eternity*. Vol. 17, May, 1966, reprinted by permission.
7. Tournier, P. *The Person Reborn*. New York: Harper & Row, 1966, p. 205.
8. When a rough draft of this chapter was discussed by a group of psychologists and psychology students, there was considerable debate about whether a chapter on pride should even be included. Several felt that pride is always an expres-

sion of inferiority and that two separate chapters were not necessary. If pride and inferiority really refer to the same condition, we may have some explanation for the Bible's emphasis on pride but silence on inferiority.

9. Graham, op. cit., p. 19.
10. Proverbs 21:4; James 4:6; I John 2:16.
11. Proverbs 6:16,17.
12. Proverbs 16:18.
13. Fromm, E. *The Heart of Man: Its Genius for Good and Evil.* New York: Harper & Row, 1964.
14. Ibid., p. 74.
15. See footnote 10.
16. Proverbs 6:16, 17.
17. I Peter 5:5; Micah 6:8; James 4:6-10.
18. I John 1:9.
19. James 4:10; I Peter 5:5,6.
20. Romans 12:3.

CHAPTER 7

Envy

According to an ancient legend there once was a young Greek athlete who competed at the public games and lost. The crowd acclaimed the winner and decided to erect a great statue in his honor. The loser, filled with envy, decided he would destroy the statue. Every night under the cover of darkness he went out and chiseled at the base in an attempt to weaken the statue's foundation. Finally he succeeded and the sculpture toppled, but it fell on the disgruntled athlete, who died a victim of his own envy.

Envy is an emotion that everybody possesses but to which nobody admits. While many people would confess that they are anxious, discouraged, lonely, overly busy or bothered by feelings of inferiority, very few of us will tell another we are envious. Indeed, we don't even like to admit this to ourselves. But above all, we especially want to keep our envy a secret from the person whom we envy.

Several years ago a massive book on envy was written by a sociologist and published in Germany.[1] In this volume the author convincingly demonstrated that envy is characteristic of people in societies the world over, but he also concluded that envy is much more destructive than most of us would care to admit. This conclusion has been echoed by evangelist Billy Graham who once wrote that envy can "ruin reputations, split churches, and cause murders. Envy can shrink our circle of friends, ruin our business, and dwarf our souls. . . .I have never seen a man who profited in any way by being envious of others," Dr. Graham continues, "but I have seen hundreds cursed by it."[2]

The Bible gives many illustrations of the prevalence and destructive power of envy. Cain, largely because of his envy, murdered his brother Abel. The Philistines, envious of Isaac's possessions, filled his wells with dirt. Joseph was sold into slavery by his envious brothers. Because they envied his popularity and power, the religious leaders of Jesus' day criticized the Lord's actions, questioned His credentials, discounted His miracles, excommunicated a blind man whom He had healed and eventually arranged both for His murder and the imprisonment of His disciples. The Apostle Paul lists envy along with idolatry, murder, drunkenness and heresy as characteristics of men who ignore God,[3] while James bluntly states that envy and strife are always accompanied by confusion and evil actions.[4]

The Meaning of Envy

Envy is a feeling of discontent usually accompanied by ill will. This feeling arises when we see that another possesses something (such as success, special advantages cr possessions) that we do not have but would like to have. When a person is envious, he not only wants what the envied person has,[5] but also desires to see the envied person hurt, disgraced, or toppled from his position. This leads to daydreaming about what it would be like if our wishes were fulfilled. Envy is like a cancer which slowly and subtly takes over a person's thinking so that "the envious man feels others' fortunes are his misfortunes; their profit, his loss; their blessing, his bane; their health, his illness; their promotion, his demotion; their success, his failure."[6]

Envy involves making comparisons, but to compare is not always to envy. A man can compare himself along with his accomplishments to another man and yet feel no envy. Remember the proud Pharisee who prayed aloud in the temple? I have compared myself with this sinner, the Pharisee said in essence, but I don't envy him. In fact, I'm glad that I am not like him.[7]

Technically speaking, envy also differs from begrudging, coveting, emulating, and feeling jealousy although these concepts are related, often used together, and sometimes seen as synonyms. To *begrudge* is to want another man not to have the honors and possessions that he deserves.

Sometimes, for example, a deacon might begrudge the pastor's status and position of leadership. To *covet* is to long for another person's possessions including his money, power, prestige, or (according to the Ten Commandments) his wife. It is possible for us to covet something, however, and not to envy the person who possesses what we desire. I might covet a new stereo system, for example, but not envy the owner of the store who possesses several stereos. To *emulate* is to follow or to attempt to be like another. This has been called "a noble trait"[8] which involves the imitation of something excellent and the unwillingness to fall short of some desirable model. But emulation that inspires can slip into envy that destroys. This is especially likely when we fail to become like the person whom we are trying to emulate. Finally, to be *jealous* is to fear that one's possessions or position will be taken by another. The envious person lacks what he wants and is discontent because of the possessions of another. The jealous person has what he wants and he does not want to lose what he possesses.

Some jealousy is justifiable. God called Himself jealous or unwilling to have another take His position of sovereignty.[9] More often jealousy is unjustifiable and involves a feeling of threat and malice because some other person is competing with us and in a position to outshine or overpower us. In almost all of these examples there is an element of selfishness in which the person wants something solely or primarily for himself.

The Sources of Envy

Some psychologists regard envy as inborn—an emotion that exists from the beginning of life and must be controlled.[10] Others believe that envy is a learned characteristic which children pick up early in life.[11] While there is still debate about the source of envy, we do know that some people have more envy in them than others. There are at least three reasons for this.

First, envy is especially prevalent in people who feel they are failures. When a person tries something and doesn't succeed as he had hoped, he becomes envious of other people who have succeeded. This was the problem of the unsuccessful Greek athlete whom we described at the beginning of the chapter. The winner didn't feel envious. This emotion was reserved for the man who tried hard but still didn't get to be number one. This struggle to be superior often arises in the home when children struggle with each other or with other members of the family in an attempt to outshine each other and be successful.

Whether a person considers himself a success depends on his definition of the word. Some people have goals in life which are so high that they are unattainable. They are never satisfied, but are always unhappy because they don't have more. Thus they are inclined to envy.

Closely related to this is a second reason for the prevalence of envy. Envy is almost always an expression of inferiority. Consciously or unconsciously the envious person considers himself inferior to other men and he doesn't like being in this position. Surely this was Saul's problem when he returned home following a battle with the Philistines. "Saul has slain his thousands," the crowd shouted, "and David his ten thousands." This cry angered Saul who must have felt inferior to David, afraid of him, and envious of the young man who had become so popular with the multitudes.[12]

Inferiority is often accompanied by the belief that we have been deprived of something which we justly deserve. An envious Cain must have felt inferior to his brother and resentful because Abel got the recognition from God that Cain wanted and felt he deserved. A similar situation characterized Jacob and Esau, for here the older brother felt he was inferior to the younger and unjustly deprived of status and honor. The same is true with envious men and women today. They frequently harbor feelings of inferiority and believe that they have been unjustly deprived.

Thirdly, envy is a sin which most often occurs in people who are far from God. The man who ignores the words of Christ is characterized by envy.[13] The envious man shows a characteristic that should be avoided because it is Satanic, linked with malice and other sin, and described bluntly as "being rotten."[14] Psychological writers support the Biblical statements and maintain that envy is closely associated with many troublesome characteristics including uncontrolled anger, grief, hostility, aggression, self-pity and guilt.[15]

The Influence of Envy

Envy is more than a troublesome emotion. It is a characteristic which can greatly influence our whole way of behavior. It affects whole societies. Sometimes governments fall and kings are replaced because of the envy of those who want to be leaders. Political parties compete against each other to some extent because each envies the success or power which might go to another. Social critics dream of great and good societies where everyone will be equal and envy will be gone, but such utopias are impossible this side of heaven because man always finds something new to envy and want.

But envy also influences individuals. It affects our thinking so that we look for faults in the people whom we envy and rejoice when they fall. It influences our speech and leads us to gossip, criticize and spread rumors that can harm another's reputation—and humor has sharply pointed up the truth:

> I hate the guys who minimize and criticize the other guys whose enterprise has made them rise above the guys who criticize.[16]

Envy affects our feelings since the person who is envious and critical cannot be joyful, happy, or contented. Even our actions are affected by envy. Meanness, revenge, delinquency, violence, and even murder or suicide have all been shown to stem from envy.[17]

Many of the problems that church members

have in getting along with each other can also result from envy. We may become envious, for example, because some other church is growing faster than ours, some other preacher is better than ours, some other Christian is more spiritual than we are, some Sunday school teacher is more dynamic than ours, or some person is more influential than we are. Recently I talked with a missionary about the problems of the mission field. The biggest problems in our mission, he said, are loneliness, discouragement and envy. Apparently some missionaries feel threatened and unable to tolerate situations in which another missionary is more successful. Regretfully, the witness and effectiveness of the local church can be wiped out because the congregation is filled with believers who envy one another and are more concerned about this than about witnessing or serving Christ as He has commanded.

It's plain that envy can hinder our getting along with other people. When we envy a person, we are likely to feel uncomfortable, inferior, angry, and perhaps guilty when we are in his presence. We are on guard lest we reveal our envy but we are always searching in hopes of finding some fault with our adversary. Little wonder one writer has concluded that "envy isolates one from his fellow man," and that "the envious man is destined to live alone."[18]

What is worse, however, is that envy separates us from God. As we have seen, envy is a sin and the Scriptures are clear in stating that the man who harbors sin in his life has a gulf between himself and God.[19]

The Control of Envy

What can we do to manage envy? Psychology is not very helpful in answering this question. There are relatively few discussions of envy in psychological literature; what little there is indicates small hope for doing much to control or eliminate it. One writer has suggested that the problem of envy is partially solved by "significant people who influence the thinking of children and adults," but there is no elaboration of how all of this is to be done and the author seems to think that if envy were really eliminated or even reduced significantly the whole society would collapse.[20]

There are, however, several ways we can tackle envy. First, understand the nature of envy. Understanding is a basic step in dealing with any problem. When we know what envy is, why it arises and how it affects us, we can be more alert to its dangers, more aware of its scope and better able to rid it from our lives. If envy arises out of our feelings of inferiority, we can apply the principles discussed in Chapter 5 and we can seek, perhaps with the help of a counselor, to find areas where we are able to succeed and be recognized. Also, since envy is a sin, we can confess it to God, recognizing that divine forgiveness is promised to those who are repentant.[21]

Second, we can deal with envy by recognizing its prevalence. Envy is a universal attitude. If we are bothered by envy we gain nothing by feeling sorry for ourselves, by dwelling on our guilt, or by moping because we have such a thorn in the flesh. Everyone struggles with envy. We might as well face that fact, agree that we are not unique or especially despicable and then get on with the job of doing something about our envious feelings.

A third step, one that tends to be overlooked, is that we should rely on divine strength to help us overcome our envy. By ourselves it is difficult to change envious behavior, but God is powerful. His Son has all the strength that we need to overcome envy. This is why the Scripture could say that with God nothing is impossible and that we can do all things through the strength that Christ gives.[22]

A fourth way to deal with envy is to accept the sovereignty and wisdom of God. It is not hard to accept God's will when He gives us what we want or puts us in a desirable position. If other people envy us, we might think, "That's too bad—for them, but after all God has put us where He wants to. . ." It is much more difficult to be content when God gives us less than we want or when He puts us in an unenviable position. This is also why it is difficult to accept defeat graciously or to fail in a task.

Never forget, however, that a God who is all-knowing and all-powerful gives us the abilities, responsibilities and position in life that He wants us to have.[23] Our task, then, is not to envy others who seem to have something different or something more. Instead, we must acknowledge God's wisdom in putting us where we are and we must be concerned more about spiri-

tual things than our earthly status and possessions.[24] This cannot be criticized as an overly
simplistic solution to a complex problem. If we
are truly concerned about serving God and
absolutely convinced of His power, sovereignty
and wisdom, there will be no need for time or
effort spent in worrying and griping because
someone else is better off than we are.

This, of course, is not meant to excuse inactivity or to give us reason for procrastination
or laziness. We could conclude that God did not
give us much so He probably doesn't expect
much and as a result we refuse to do much. On
the contrary, God expects us to be the best that
we can be and to do all that we can do with the
abilities and opportunities we've got.

As in the parable of the vineyard workers, [25]
some people seem to have it better than others.
We might not be wholly satisfied with our place
in life, but malice, criticism, anger, and self-pity
are not the right responses. Instead, let us realize
that an all-wise, all-knowing God has given us
the privilege of serving where we are. This is
cause not for envy but for increased diligence,
rejoicing, and thanksgiving.

Questions for Further Thought and Discussion

1. According to this chapter "Envy is an emotion that
   everybody possesses but to which nobody admits."
   What makes you envious? What are the causes of
   envy in others?
2. How does envy differ from comparing, begrudging,
   coveting, emulating and jealousy?
3. Is envy always bad? Give reasons for your answer.

4. How does envy affect most people?

5. How does it affect *you*?

6. What can you do about the envy in your life? Will your suggested solution *really* work?

7. Can envy always be eliminated or do we sometimes just have to live with it?

8. According to the Scriptures, God gives each of us certain abilities and status in life (see footnote 23). Is it sinful, therefore, to have ambitions and to strive for something better?

Footnotes

1. Schoeck, H. *Envy: A Theory of Social Behavior.* New York: Harcourt, Brace & World, Inc., 1969.
2. Graham, B. *Seven Deadly Sins.* Grand Rapids: Zondervan, 1955, p. 41-42.
3. Galatians 5:19-21.
4. James 3:16.
5. The element of wanting is stressed by psychoanalytic and other writers as being a vital part of envy (see Joffe, W.G., An Unenviable Preoccupation with Envy. *Psychiatry and Social Science Review.* Vol. 4, December, 1970, pp. 12-21) but Schoeck (*op. cit., 1969, p. 5*) in contrast, claims that the envier "almost never" wants for himself what the envied person possesses. The reader can decide which of these views is correct. The author inclines to the former: the envier wants!
6. Flynn, L. B. *You Can Live Above Envy.* Wheaton, Illinois: Conservative Baptist Press, 1970, p. 21.
7. Luke 18:9-12.
8. Flynn, op. cit., p. 17.
9. Exodus 20:5.
10. Klein, M. *Envy and Gratitude: A Study of Unconscious Sources.* New York: Basic Books 1957.
11. Joffe, op. cit.
12. I Samuel 18:6-12.
13. I Timothy 6:3,4.
14. Romans 13:13; James 3:14-16; Titus 3:3; Galatians 5:19-21,26; Proverbs 14:30.
15. See Joffe, op. cit.; Schoech, op. cit.; and Horney, K. *The Neurotic Personality of Our Time.* New York: W. W. Norton, 1937.
16. Flynn, op. cit., p. 48.

17. Schoeck, op. cit., **chapter 8, and Flynn,** op. cit., **page 50ff.**
18. Graham, op. cit., p. 41.
19. Isaiah 59:1,2; Psalm 66:18.
20. Schoeck, op. cit., **Chapter 17.**
21. I John 1:9.
22. Luke 1:37; Philippians 4:13.
23. I Corinthians 12; Romans 12; Ephesians 4:8-12.
24. Colossians 3:1-2; Matthew 6:19-21.
25. Matthew 20:1-16.

CHAPTER 8

Loneliness

Admiral Richard E. Byrd, the famous explorer, once published a fascinating little book describing his experiences during the several months he spent alone at the weather base in the Antarctic. Originally Byrd had looked forward to the solitude, but once he settled into his frigid accommodation he found himself longing to be with other people. "This morning I had to admit to myself that I was lonely," he wrote in his diary. "Try as I may, I find I can't take my loneliness casually. It is too big. I must not dwell on it; otherwise I am undone."[1] The psalmist, centuries before, experienced something similar: "Hear my prayer, O Lord," he cried, "I am like a pelican of the wilderness: I am like an owl of the desert. I watch, and as a sparrow alone upon the house top."[2]

When we consider loneliness, our minds often think of people who, like Admiral Byrd and the writer of this Psalm, are isolated in secluded places. But it is also possible to be lonely, intensely lonely, when we are surrounded by people. My first visit to London came when I was a student who had gone overseas to study for a year. This was an exciting time in my life but I can still remember the first day. "There are eight million people in this city," I wrote in my travel diary, "and not one of them knows or cares about me." I felt like the lonely foreigner whom Paul Tournier describes in one of his books.[3] Each evening this lady would turn on the radio just to hear an announcer say, "We bid you a very pleasant good night!" It wasn't very personal, but at least it was a human voice in the midst of loneliness.

But one need not even travel to another country to feel lonely. Many people feel isolated and lonely in their own community, in their own places of work, in their own churches, and in their own homes. Loneliness affects old and young alike. It influences those who don't know very many people and those whose lives are in constant contact with others. It affects the poor and the rich. It is a problem for unbelievers and Christians.

The Causes of Loneliness

When people live in solitude like Admiral Byrd at the South Pole, it is not difficult to understand their feelings of isolation and loneliness. But why should anyone be lonely when there are other people around? Why should Billy Graham conclude, as he did recently, that loneliness is the one problem that plagues more people these days than any other?[4] Why should Paul Tournier, the Christian psychiatrist, call loneliness "the most devastating malady of this age"?[5] Answers to these questions can be grouped in two categories. First, man is lonely when he is cut off from other men, and second, he is lonely because of his separation from God.

To say that man is lonely because he is cut off from other men doesn't explain much unless you can understand why man is cut off in the first place. Why should a person get so separated from other people that he feels isolated? First, some men are separated from others because of their position as leaders. Others may be near—friends, supporters and followers—but a leader must be ahead of and hence apart from others.

> If the leader is defined as walking ahead of the group, he is necessarily separated from the group, alone, isolated. , .unoriginal followers can hardly appreciate original leadership. . .every act of courage and every creative initiative tends to isolate the leader. Whoever goes first goes, by definition, alone.[6]

It should be emphasized, however, that to be alone and out in front does not always mean that one is lonely. A lot of people are alone in positions of leadership but they are not lonely because they have managed to find useful and satisfying ways to fill their free hours.[7]

A second and more common reason for separation and resulting loneliness is the tendency to reject others. Some of us feel lonely because, consciously or unconsciously, we have cast aside the friendship and companionship of other people. Sometimes we do this because of pride. When a man is greatly impressed with his own importance or his own superiority, he has difficulty communicating with others or building warm relationships with those whom he considers to be his inferior. This happens sometimes with Christians. We develop a spiritual pride and become so impressed with our own importance we refuse to fellowship with anybody who differs from us. Once we have cut everybody else off, we remain isolated in our pride and loneliness.

Closely related to this love of self is a hostility towards other people. The person who is critical, sarcastic, and opposed to others; the man who is inconsiderate and unloving; and the individual who doesn't care about others, will soon find himself alone. Highly critical people sometimes develop friendships with others who are equally critical and complaining but for the most part the hostile man is a lonely man.

Then there is fear. Sometimes we reject others and refuse to get near them because we are afraid of them. We might want desperately to be close but because we don't know how to act in the presence of others we cower by ourselves, remaining lonely and at a safe distance from the very people who could remove our loneliness. This is seen frequently in young children who, when they arrive in the presence of other children, stand by themselves in a corner watching the play. The child who stands alone may want to be a part of the action but he doesn't know how to relate to the other children or how to get into the group.

This brings us to the matter of self-hatred. Sometimes, because of our inferiority feelings or self-critical attitudes, we conclude that nobody would want to spend time with us. Convinced that we are worthless and that people do not find us attractive, we stay by ourselves and refuse to get close to others, even though we might desperately want to be accepted.

A third reason why we are separated from other men is that people sometimes reject us. In this case, loneliness is forced upon us. Sometimes little children are lonely because they have been ignored or rejected by adults who are disinterested or too busy doing something else. Teenagers often feel lonely when they are criticized by adults, unsuccessful in their struggles to be accepted by peers, or desperately wanting to make it in a society that still values success more than anything else. Married people often find themselves lonely, rejected, or ignored by spouses who have forgotten the excitement of the honeymoon and become too busy with things outside the home. Single adults and divorced people are often the loneliest members of the community because there is no place for them in the society, and usually no real place for them in the church. In addition, middle-aged people whose children leave, grief-stricken relatives, and forsaken old people, are all inclined to be lonely because they have been left by themselves. Do you remember the poignant cry of King David?

> Cast me not off in the time of old age? Forsake me
> not when my strength faileth. When I am old and
> greyheaded, O God, Forsake me not.[8]

When a man has cut himself off from others his loneliness is self-imposed and perhaps more tolerable, but the man who has been forsaken has a loneliness which is especially depressing.

The inability to keep up with other people and with a changing society is another reason why men are separated from each other and, hence, lonely. A generation ago, loneliness was probably less common than it is today. More people lived in small communities where everyone knew everyone else and where people felt more needed. Today most of our population live in congested cities where we often don't even know the neighbors. One quarter of the U.S. population moves every year so we are less inclined and less able to develop lasting friendships. With technological advances we are less dependent on our neighbor and he is less in need of us. In a society where we evaluate a man more on the basis of what he can do than on what or who he is, many people feel dehumanized, worthless, unneeded, or ignored, and hence very lonely.

We should realize, however, that some people like to be alone—to spend time by themselves. By His example and preaching, Jesus taught that periods of solitude are good, refreshing, and probably even necessary if people are to function effectively. But a voluntary drawing apart for a temporary period of solitude is not the same as being lonely. One writer has suggested that loneliness and solitude are really very different. "Loneliness," he writes, "is negative; solitude can be positive. . . .Loneliness speaks of the pain of being alone; solitude expresses the glory of being alone. Loneliness (is). . .the acute chronic non-directed sense of aloneness (and loss of self-esteem) that breaks down man's integration!. . .Solitude can. . .be a glorious experience."[9] The glory of solitude was Jesus' experience as He frequently withdrew from the crowd and went to the hills to pray.

Although loneliness often arises because we are separated from other men, it can also come when we are separated from God. In an oft-quoted prayer, Augustine expressed man's need for God: "Thou hast formed us for Thyself and our hearts are restless till they find rest in Thee." God made man for Himself but man rebelled against his Creator and cut himself off from God and His glory.[10] Separated from divine companionship, man is incomplete, restless, and lonely.

The Cures of Loneliness

Many people have suggested solutions to the problem of loneliness. Most common are the admonitions to be active, to do something in order to fill up time and to get our minds off our own isolation. Richard Wolff has summarized some of these admonitions. They

. . .never cease: change jobs, join a club, be positive, become aggressive, get married, get remarried,

travel, move, have fun, never be alone, use the
record player, listen to the radio, watch television,
enjoy the movies, read a good book, take up a
hobby, pursue cultural interests, expand your hori-
zons, play, go to church, live a little, remember
sex, start working, increase leisure, develop hobbies, renew goals, volunteer. . .

But then the author adds, correctly I believe,
"All of these activities may temporarily remedy
the pain of loneliness but they fail to meet the
problem on the deepest level and do not produce the desired lasting result."[11]

A different solution to the problem of loneliness has been offered by a psychologist named
Clark Moustakas who suggests that we should
learn to see loneliness as something positive. [12]
Why not look for the good in loneliness, he asks,
recognizing that it really brings deeper percep-
tion, greater sensitivity, and increased insight
into one's own being? Certainly there can be
value in looking for the bright side in all of our
experiences. God permits problems to arise for
our own good at times and loneliness may be
one of these problems. But loneliness can't be
defeated by pretending that it is something
wonderful. It isn't wonderful. It is painful and
often unbearable and it doesn't help much if we
pretend otherwise.

A more realisitic solution to the problem of
loneliness has been offered by the noted psychoanalyst Eric Fromm.[13] When men are lonely,
Fromm says (and in his opinion loneliness is
almost universal), man must somehow unite with
other people. We must develop "productive

love"—a love that is characterized by mutual care, respect, and understanding. The recent popularity of sensitivity groups and communes reflect man's attempt to unite with other men. By sharing possessions, ideas, feelings, aspirations, problems, and even bodies, many lonely people experience the rare closeness for which they long. The recent interest in Eastern religions, free sex, drug experiences, and mysticism all indicate a struggle to overcome loneliness and to unite with other people or with some unknown cosmic being. In churches there is a re-emphasis on the importance of small groups, a reaction against a tendency to be cold, impersonal, and lacking in real love for other people in the congregation.

Fromm has made a second suggestion concerning how we can overcome loneliness: we can submit to a human authority. Many people today are confused by the changes which are taking place in society and frustrated over their inability to keep up and find meaning in life. As some, in desperation, are trying to destroy and bring down this mixed-up establishment, others are looking for a new leader who will demonstrate that he can bring law and order out of chaos. Let such a leader appear and millions will follow, hoping for security and mutual involvement in a movement that will give them a purpose in living, contact with others, and freedom from loneliness. Fromm points out that this partially explains the success of Hitler. He rallied a group of followers together around a common cause.

This might have eliminated their loneliness for a while but it illustrates an important warning that applies to all of these suggested cures. Just because something eliminates loneliness does not necessarily make it good. Following Hitler may have reduced the lonely feelings in many German people, but the cure was worse than the original disease. The various solutions proposed may all have some value in helping people to overcome their loneliness, but they all ignore man's separation from God. This is really at the base of all human loneliness.

Although God has promised to be a constant companion,[14] many refuse this. They prefer instead to remain on their own, separated from God. This even happens to Christians. We accept Christ into our lives but then we push Him into a place of unimportance where we ignore Him, refuse His fellowship, and then complain about our loneliness. Submission to God, therefore, is necessary if we are to overcome our real feelings of isolation.

This important step in overcoming loneliness is not the only step, however. Sometimes churchgoers enthusiastically sing a hymn which includes the words, "Why should I be lonely? I have Jesus only." But these words forget about Adam. He had divine companionship but God said that Adam needed to have fellowship with another human being.[15] In the Garden of Gethsemane Jesus was well aware of His Father's presence but in addition the Lord seemed to need His disciples nearby.[16] Paul, in his prison cell, must have been aware of God's presence but he longed for the companionship of Timothy and Mark.[17]

Companionship with other humans is necessary for everyone and is a natural outgrowth of our submission to Christ. In Galatians 5 we read about the fruit of the Spirit. Many of the characteristics of committed believers are traits that enable us to get along with others: love, peace, patience, gentleness and goodness, for example. When these become part of our lives, through the work of the Holy Spirit, we are able to relate to others in sincerity and with genuine interest. In turn, others respond positively to us. This is not to imply that when we submit to Christ, friendships will arise spontaneously and loneliness will disappear automatically. There are additional ways to handle loneliness. These include working to get along with people, learning to communicate, striving to remove the pride of self-condemnation which alienates us from other people, and actively getting involved in helping others, feeling useful and needed. With all of this we must be yielded to the living God and guided by His Holy Spirit. Only then are we really able to meet the problem of loneliness.

Questions for Further Thought and Discussion

1. Do you know people who are lonely? Who are they? Are there lonely people in your church?
2. Why do people feel lonely?
3. What sorts of things make *you* feel lonely?
4. Can people be lonely without realizing it?
5. Is it wrong for a Christian to be lonely? (See II Timothy 4:16, 17 and John 16:32; then look at Genesis 2:18 and II Timothy 4:9-11.)

6. List specific and practical action we can take to get rid of loneliness. Will the suggestions on your list really work—even when loneliness comes because others have rejected you?
7. Is there practical action you can take to help lonely people in your church or community feel less lonely?

Footnotes

1. Byrd, R. E. *Alone*, New York: Putnam, 1938.
2. Psalm 102:1,6,7.
3. Tournier, P. *Escape from Loneliness*. Philadelphia: The Westminster Press, 1962, p. 13.
4. Graham, B. "Loneliness: How It Can Be Cured." *Readers' Digest*, October, 1969. p. 135.
5. Tournier, op. cit.
6. Wolff, R. *Man At The Top*. Wheaton, Illinois: Tyndale House, 1969, p. 71-2.
7. Billy Graham, op. cit., who is certainly a leader, has emphasized this point. All leaders are alone, but only some are lonely.
8. Psalm 71:9,18.
9. Wolff, R. *The Meaning of Loneliness*. Wheaton, Illinois: Key Publishers, 1970, p. 94.
10. Romans 3:23.
11. Wolff, op. cit., p. 45.
12. Moustakas, C. *Loneliness*. Englewood Cliff, New Jersey: Prentice Hall, 1961.
13. Fromm, E. *Escape from Freedom*. New York: Rinehart, 1941.
14. Joshua 1:9; Isaiah 43:2; Psalm 23:4; Matthew 28:20b.
15. Genesis 2:18.
16. Matthew 26:36-45.
17. II Timothy 4:9-11, 16, 17, 21.

CHAPTER 9

Busyness

When I graduated from college, it was customary to have our pictures published in the school yearbook along with a statement of our undergraduate achievements and a quotation from some prominent figure. I can still remember the quotation that was chosen by one of my fellow classmates. It was a short little verse by William Henry Davies:

> What is this life
> If so full of care
> We have no time
> To stand and stare?

Clutching our diplomas and finally out from under the heavy hands of our professors, most of us, I am sure, hoped that we would at least have time to relax, to stand and to stare. Perhaps some of my classmates did go forth to lives that are leisurely, relaxing and unhurried, but for most of us in the 1970s, life is not like that. It is full of care, pressure, and an endless round of frenzied activity. "I am too busy," is not only an excuse for avoiding involvement in something we do not want to do, it is a description of our whole way of life. This is a strange country, wrote a couple of psychologists several years ago,

> . . .where the inhabitants run as hard as they can in order to hold their own. It seems particularly queer in a country where the standard of living is so bounteous and the apparatus for leisure activity so highly elaborated. Yet growing affluence and increasing opportunities for leisure have done little to diminish the American's feeling of being under pressure. . . .It often seems that among job, family, (church) and community activities, at least thirty hours a day are firmly committed.[1]

As members of a rushing society, many of us are caught up in a treadmill of busyness. Perhaps we ought to be asking why.

The Causes of Busyness

Numerous articles and books have been written about anxiety, discouragement, loneliness, anger, and some of the other topics that have been discussed in this book, but very little has been written about busyness—the hyperactivity that seems to characterize so many modern men. In the absence of published commentaries on this problem and a large body of research, we can only speculate why people are so busy. Undoubtedly the reasons are complex and varied, but for any one person, some of the following explanations probably hold true.

First, people are busy because of a desire to conform and be accepted. Several years ago, psychologist Robert Lindner suggested that the pressure to conform has become an eleventh commandment in our society.[2] We stress it in childrearing, it becomes the slogan of political parties, and it is a rule which applies to the members of many churches. Young people in our society are sick of this, but in their criticism of conformity they themselves often conform in behavior, dress and speech to other so-called nonconformists.

Why should people try so hard to conform? There are two reasons. First, when we conform, we are most likely to be accepted by others. The nonconformist is often considered to be highly individualistic and few of us want that kind of a reputation. Thus in our struggle to be accepted, we conform to what others expect. Secondly, when others accept us (partially as a result of our willingness to conform), we can more easily accept ourselves. The unceasing struggle to conform, the attempts to do what other people expect, and the worry about how others will react to us, may all be indirect attempts to acquire self-acceptance.

Let's look at some examples. In many universities, faculty members are expected to publish regular books and articles in their field. In their effort to meet this expectation and keep their jobs, these professors work consistently on their research and books. By doing this they are more likely to be accepted by the dean and other faculty members, promoted to a higher rank and salary, and able, because of the acceptance of others, to more easily accept themselves. Closer to home, in many neighborhoods the residents work busily in their yards, not only because they like the yard to look good, but because all the neighbors expect it. If I keep my lawn cut, my neighbors will approve of me and I can more easily approve of myself as a member of the community. Again, in church many believers conform to accepted standards and ways of behavior, not primarily from devotion to God or because these traditions are biblical, but rather because the pastor and other church members will approve and this enables the conformist to more easily accept himself.

A second reason for busyness is our desire to keep up with a changing society. With advancing technology things are changing faster and faster and it is getting more and more difficult to keep abreast of what's happening. In *Alice In Wonderland*, the queen had some words which might very well apply today. "Here," she said, "it takes all the running you can do (just) to keep in the same place. If you want to get some place else, you must run at least twice as fast as that!" Like the fictional people in Alice's dream world, we have become a nation of individuals who are running as hard as we can just to keep up. And the race will probably get faster. As the society changes more rapidly, we are going to have to increase our pace accordingly.

A compulsive desire to escape from the problems of life becomes the third cause for busyness. When a person loses a loved one, life often becomes empty, meaningless and filled with despair. There are several ways in which people react to such grief, but one way is to get active. By keeping busy, the grief-stricken person is able to forget the loss and the emptiness, at least temporarily. Might it be that much of our busyness today is an escape—a way for avoiding the anxiety, emptiness, guilt, discouragement, and loneliness we have discussed in previous chapters?

Busyness helps us to escape the problems of life in at least three ways. First, it helps to fill the vacuum and avoid the emptiness that characterizes so many of our lives. After throwing out God, many people have substituted a cycle of frenzied activities and numerous projects (many of which may be worthwhile) to fill the gap and prevent them from facing their frustrations, futility and lack of values in life. Secondly, busyness helps people to avoid responsibility. If we can convince others that we really are very busy, then we have a good excuse for not taking on additional projects and obligations. Activity can hide the fact that we are lazy and unwilling to put forth the effort to do worthwhile projects. Thirdly, busyness lets us deceive ourselves and others into thinking that we are very important since we have so many projects that put demands on our time.

It is also probable that for many people busyness is primarily an expression of tension. Most people have at some time had the experience of feeling anxious—before an important job interview, before making a speech, or perhaps before getting married. When we get tense like this, we often pace up and down, squirm in a chair or move our hands and feet nervously. Many people today are running their lives on nervous energy. They are tense, uptight people who simply do not know how to unwind.

How do people get tense in the first place? In a society that worships success, some people become tense and worried because they are afraid of failure. This is especially true when a person has failed before or is convinced that he is no good. Such a man waits in tense anticipation for the time when he will fail again. Others may have learned to be tense by watching parents and heeding adult warnings that they must conform and push themselves to get ahead in life. For these people, busyness and tension have become habits which have been picked up and cannot be dropped. Most of us have been born, it seems, on a merry-go-round that is running faster and faster. Like the writer of the popular song, many other people wish they could shout out: "Stop the world, I want to get off."

The Cost of Busyness

When man was created many centuries ago, God decreed that we should rest one day a week.[3] Apparently, the Creator was telling us that we needed periodic rejuvenation, that we could not rush on forever. There is now scientific evidence to show that perpetual busyness, while it may help us to get a lot done, also takes a heavy toll.

First, it takes its toll physically. We know that hyperactivity (that is, busyness) and tension can produce ulcers and sometimes create permanent damage in the stomach and intestines, high blood pressure which can damage the heart or blood vessels and make the person more susceptible to heart attacks, asthma and other breathing difficulties, migraine headaches, and a variety of other ailments. We can buoy ourselves up with all kinds of pills and energizers, but eventually the body that is pushed unduly will break down.

Busyness also takes its toll psychologically. Most of us realize that if we do not get enough rest, we become inefficient and difficult to live with. Within recent years, this has been studied scientifically. One recent study has shown, for example, that consistent activity and insufficient sleep slows down reaction time, decreases alertness so that we cannot think clearly, brings impairment of memory, and sometimes even leads to mental breakdowns.[4] Communist brainwashers in Korea during the action there were well aware of this need for sleep and dreaming, for one of the ways they wore down prisoners was to prevent them from getting consistent rest. Eventually the prisoners of war could not think clearly, could not resist the pressure of the interrogators, and sometimes signed confessions that they would not have signed otherwise.

Excessive busyness also takes its toll socially. When we are so involved in busy activity that we do not get enough rest or relaxation, we often become short-tempered. We find it harder to be nice to others, to tolerate behavior that we do not like in others, or be patient in dealing with other people. Books on communication often point out that to effectively communicate takes time. When we are too busy to take this time, our relationships with others deteriorate. Often we do not have time to help people who are in need or to give them support and encouragement.

Fourth, busyness influences us spiritually. When Christians get busy, one of the first things to drop out of their schedule is a time spent in prayer and Bible study. This is even true of theology students and busy pastors who sometimes assume that because of their church attendance and study of theology they can eliminate or cut back on their time with God. Sometimes we get very busy, even in Christian work, and fail to realize that this activity is keeping us away from God. Then, without being aware of what is happening, we begin to slide spiritually.

Dealing with Busyness

If frenzied activity is so harmful, the solution is obvious: we have to slow down. This could mean a total stoppage—doing nothing. But for most people, slowing down is easier said than done. If we have correctly analyzed the causes of busyness, to slow down means that we risk rejection by others, falling behind socially or having to face up to personal problems we would prefer to avoid. Furthermore, if we stop being busy, we might just let tensions build up inside. This bottling up of feelings could do as much harm as the busyness we are trying to escape.

Is there any escape? How can we find a compromise solution that will enable us to reduce our pace but still satisfy the needs our busyness now meets?

Several years ago, Dr. Charles Hummel, the busy president of Barrington College in Rhode Island, tackled this problem in a little booklet entitled *Tyranny of the Urgent*. Have you wished for a thirty-four hour day? he asked. If you had it, would that really solve the busyness problem?

> We live in constant tension between the urgent and the important. The problem is that the important task rarely must be done today, or even this week. Extra hours of prayer and Bible study, a visit with that non-Christian friend, careful study of an important book: these projects can wait. But the urgent tasks call for instant action—endless demands pressure every hour and day.

> A man's home is no longer his castle; it is no longer a place away from urgent tasks because the telephone breaches the walls with imperious demands. The momentary appeal of these tasks seems irresistible and important and they devour our energy. But in the light of time's perspective their deceptive prominence fades; with a sense of loss we recall the important tasks pushed aside. We realize that we've become slaves to the tyranny of the urgent.

> Is there any escape from this pattern of living? The answer lies in the life of our Lord. . . .The Gospel record shows that Jesus worked hard. . .yet His life was never feverish. . . .His life showed a wonderful balance, a sense of timing. . . .

What was the secret of Jesus' work? We find a clue following Mark's account of Jesus' busy day. Mark observes that " . . . in the morning, a great while before day, He rose and went out to a lonely place, and there He prayed" (Mark 1:35). Here is the secret of Jesus' life and work for God: *He prayerfully waited for His Father's instructions* and for the strength to follow them. Jesus had no divinely-drawn blueprint; He discerned the Father's will day by day in a life of prayer. By this means He warded off the urgent, and accomplished the important. . .

Many of us have experienced Christ's deliverance from the penalty of sin. Are we letting Him free us from the tyranny of the urgent? He points the way: "If you *continue* in my Word." This is the way to freedom. Through prayerful meditation in God's Word, we gain His perspective. . .

Prayerful waiting on God is indispensible to effective service. Like the time-out in the football game, it enables us to catch our breath and fix new strategy. As we wait for directions the Lord frees us from the tyranny of the urgent.[5]

To escape the tyranny of the urgent and to handle the busyness of life, we must attempt to change our lives in at least two ways.

First, we must take time to evaluate our activities and organize our time. Dr. Hummel recommends that we reserve a few minutes each day, an hour every week, and a day or most of a day each month, during which we take inventory of our lives, evaluate the past, and plan for the future. When God told man to rest every seventh day, I wonder if such self-evaluation was to be a part of the Lord's day activities, instead of the frenzied Sunday programs which characterize the "day of rest" for so many people? Regardless of the amount of time we spend on evaluation, it is surely important that we regularly plan our activities more carefully and pray for guidance from the Holy Spirit so that we may be free from the tyranny of the urgent.

When we do this, an interesting by-product results—we get more done. Much of the time that was spent running around in disorganized frenzy is now spent doing planned and worthwhile things that are completed more efficiently.

A second and closely related way to attack the problem of busyness is to develop a new style of living which involves constant re-assessment of our priorities. Too often we go through life thinking that everything we do is important, that we have to complete everything we start and that we have to give in to all of the demands on our time. Too often we fail to realize that most of our present-day busyness is self-imposed.

A psychiatrist friend of mine holds the theory that people like to blame their busyness on external circumstances or on other people. We say, "I've got to," "I must," or "I can't because I don't have the time," but what this really means is that "I choose to," or "I choose not to." There is very little that we really have to do. Every time we say "I must," we are really expressing something that we have chosen to do. If we are to make the best use of our time, but not be overwhelmed by busyness, we must constantly make decisions regarding what we want or are able to do and what we should choose not to do.

This, of course, is not an easy decision. In working with seminary students, I have discovered that these men have great demands on their time. They must complete the assignments given by their professors. Many work part-time and have responsibilities in their churches. Then there is need for a personal devotional life and there are demands from their wives and families. These men must learn in seminary to establish a balance in life so that none of their various activities takes a disproportionate amount of time. The habits they establish in school will carry over to their lives out of school. The style of living that we develop now—regardless of how old we are—can carry through the rest of our lives. We must therefore constantly evaluate how much we are able to do effectively and how we can best organize our time.

God does not want His people rushing around all the time like Martha of Bethany[6] but neither does he want us always sitting around in contemplative, inactive meditation. We have a responsibility both to hear the Word of God and to be involved in useful activity.[7] The Christian who talks a lot but does nothing has a dead faith[8] and is really out of God's will. But, it would also seem that the Christian who is too busy is out of God's will. God gives us enough time to do what He wants, and if we find that we are perpetually running around in frantic activity, there is a good possibility that we have not taken the time to organize our activities and to establish priorities so that we can accomplish what God wants us to do in the time that He has made available.

If we regularly take the time to evaluate and to plan our lives in accordance with the written Word of God, our activity will be different. Life will be more productive and less hectic, more Christ-centered and less characterized by tension or pressure. It will involve better relations with others and will be characterized by a greater ability to accept ourselves. In a less frenzied and more disciplined way we will be able to conform to at least some of the social expectations of our society, to still keep aware of what is happening in our changing culture, to face our problems head-on, and to live far less tensely. We might even discover that while life may be busy and full of much care there still will be time left to "stand and to stare."

Questions for Further Thought and Discussion

1. Why are people today so busy? Can you think of answers to this question that were not mentioned by the author in the chapter?
2. What keeps you busy? Are you too busy? If so, why?
3. What is your reaction to the quotation from Dr. Hummel's booklet? Do you agree completely?
4. How do you react to the theory that we are only as busy as we choose to be—that excessive busyness is our own choosing? How does this apply to you?
5. Do you agree with the author's conclusion that the person who is too busy is really out of God's will?
6. How can people handle the problem of busyness?
7. How can you, in a practical way, deal with excessive busyness in your life?

8. It has been said that the person who is too busy is really just disorganized. Do you agree?

Footnotes

1. Putney, S. and Putney, G. J. *The Adjusted American: Normal Neurosis in the Individual and Society.* New York: Harper & Row, 1964, p. 151.
2. Lindner, R. *Must You Conform?* New York: Grove Press, 1956.
3. Exodus 16:23ff.
4. Naitoh, P. *Sleep Loss and Its Effects on Performance.* U.S. Navy Neuropsychiatric Research Unit, Report Number 68-3, 1969.
5. Hummel, C. E. *Tyranny of the Urgent.* Downers Grove, Ill.: Inter-Varsity Press, 1967, pp. 5,6,7,8,10,11.
6. Luke 10:38-42.
7. James 1:22-25; 2:14-18.
8. James 2:20, 26.

CHAPTER 10

Emptiness

In the early 1940s a successful Jewish psychiatrist, then a resident of Austria, was herded into a train with 1500 other people and sent off to a Nazi prison camp. For three grim years, prisoner number 119-104 lived in daily horror— digging trenches within the shadow of some of the giant furnaces that claimed the lives of six million Jews during World War II. Following his liberation, the psychiatrist, whose name was Victor Frankl, wrote a fascinating book about his experiences. The book was given the title *Man's Search for Meaning*, probably because one of Frankl's major conclusions after his prison experience was that men must have some meaning and purpose in life if they are to get along efficiently and (for people like Frankl in a prison camp) if they are to survive. "The prisoner who lost faith in the future," Frankl wrote of his fellow prisoners, "was doomed. With his loss of belief in the future, he also lost his spiritual hold; he let himself decline and became subject to mental and physical decay. . . . The sudden loss of hope and courage can have a deadly effect."[1]

In his writings and lectures Dr. Frankl often quoted the philosopher Nietzche who once wrote, "He who has a why to live for can bear with almost any how." In other words, the person who has a reason for living and a purpose in life can tolerate almost any difficulty. The history of Christianity and indeed the history of the world gives many examples of this. This was true of Job as he suffered many trials. It was true of Paul as he suffered during his missionary journeys. It was true of Frankl in prison at Auschwitz, and it is true for men and women today. If we have a purpose in life and a reason for living, we can bear almost anything.

For millions of people in the 1970s, however, life has no purpose or meaning. They cannot tell a reason for living. Life for them is empty. The Swiss psychiatrist, Carl Jung, recognized this several years ago when he concluded that "the central neurosis of our times is emptiness." Rollo May, a New York psychologist, once wrote that "on the basis of my clinical practice, as well as that of my psychological and psychiatric colleagues. . .the chief problem of people in the middle. . .of the twentieth century is emptiness."[2] Frankl would agree, for in his opinion "the state of inner-emptiness is at present one of the major challenges to psychiatry."[3] Visit a college campus (and many high school campuses) and you will see hundreds of people who can tell you no reasons for living. Talk to middle-aged businessmen, bored tradesmen, frustrated housewives, discouraged preachers and many thousands of people in our communities and churches and you will find lives with no real purpose—lives drifting and empty.

The Causes of Emptiness

In all of history there has probably never been as exciting a time to live as now. Every day brings news of scientific advances, new labor-saving devices, and technological changes to make life more efficient and easier. We have entertainment facilities that our grandparents never dreamed of. The most famous personalities in the world can come "in living color" into our own living rooms and, something as wonderful, if we don't want to watch, we can turn them off. But is it so amazing that in the midst of all this affluence and all of these exciting changes, there is still so much emptiness and lack of purpose in peoples' lives? Ironically, the technology that has brought so many benefits and changes to our lives is also a cause of our emptiness.

Many years ago a young man could, for example, watch his father in the blacksmith's shop or on the farm and could be pretty certain that things would be much the same when he grew up. But this is changed! Nobody can predict what life will be like even five years from now. This is one reason why parenthood and teaching are so difficult today. We don't know what to prepare young people for because nobody knows what the future will be.

I am not suggesting a return to the good old days gone by. I am simply saying that life today is much more uncertain, and that this accelerated rate of change is unavoidable. The reason for the Western world's technological superiority is that new ideas, new ways of doing things, and new styles always take first place. We are not a people clinging to outdated superstition and old-fashioned ways. Our standard of usability is to ask, "Is it new?" To make way for progress we have happily abandoned old ideas, old styles, old errors, old living standards and old habits. We have also thrown out old views of what is right and wrong. Having cast off all that seems outdated, we have very little left. Progressive modern man has no stability in the present and no certainty for the future. In other words, life is empty.

Closely connected with technological progress is a second reason for emptiness—our excess of leisure time. Recently I heard a radio commentator reading from an English law of many decades ago. Apparently the honorable members of the British Parliament reluctantly approved some legislation which limited the work week to six days and the average work day to eleven hours. The businessmen and industrial leaders of the time were appalled and described the sixty-six hour work week as "near utopia." How would these men respond if they could be here today when people have four-week vacations, numerous coffee breaks, a variety of fringe benefits and assurance that the forty-hour work week is on the way out?

Of course for numerous people, including housewives, the forty-hour work week is an unreality. Many, including professional people, students, and tradesmen, still work sixty and seventy hours each week while others fill their time with a round of frenzied activity. All of this does not hide the fact, however, that for hundreds of thousands of people there is too much time with nothing to do. Psychologists, sociologists and others are now doing research on the problem of leisure since they realize that too much time with nothing to do leads to feelings of emptiness and meaninglessness.

A third cause of emptiness is spiritual unbelief. In a little book entitled *Escape from Emptiness*, a radio preacher by the name of John D. Jess has discussed this concisely:

> The modern generation is suffering from purpose-lessness. Why?. . .Why are so many people floundering. . .? Why so much self-destruction, so many aimless drifters and frustrated searchers?
>
> The answer: *Spiritual vacuum*. When you take a cripple's crutch from him and provide no substitute, he falls. Put a man in mid-ocean without any means of staying afloat and he will drown. Rob a whole generation of its belief in God, or at least God's purpose for man, and you leave it suspended in mid-air, unsupported, unattached, direction-less.[4]

Many years ago as they were wandering through the wilderness, the nation Israel came to Mount Sinai and camped there while Moses went up into the mountain. Shortly thereafter the people began to think that Moses was lost in the hills forever and they even began to wonder if God was dead. The Biblical record of this event[5] indicates that the people simply slid into thinking that the Lord was no longer relevant. This is also what has happened to many people today, even in the church. (Remember that Israel was not a nation of pagan unbelievers—Israel was God's spokesman on earth.) Today many people, if pressed, will say, "Sure I believe in God" or "Sure He's important." Some even sing, "I love Him better every day" and "Every day with Jesus is sweeter than the day before," but in reality God may not mean much to them any more: it's entirely possible to have the form of worship without actually knowing God personally. For these people He's been replaced with an emptiness one writer has called a "vacuum of unbelief."[6]

Now, there is an elementary law of physics that states whenever a vacuum exists, something will rush in to fill the space. The ancient nation of Israel set up an idol in the form of a golden calf to fill their vacuum. In the 1970s people have set up their own idols to fill their emptiness.

Idols of the Seventies

According to the dictionary, an idol is a false god which represents a deity and is an object of devotion. This was certainly true of the golden calf in the wilderness and the wooden images that pagan people have worshiped over the centuries. Today, however, the idols we worship are much more sophisticated.

The first of these modern idols is actually a continuation of a very old one: success and status. As with most modern idols, there is nothing wrong with this in itself. Surely we should strive to be as capable, well trained, successful, and competent as we can. But success and status should not be our god. A Christian especially has a responsibility to serve the one true God; this is much more important than laying up for ourselves treasures on earth. In our society, however, it is very easy to slip into a worship of success and prestige so that this becomes the prime goal in life.

A second modern idol is the god of science. Surely no thinking person can be opposed to science; for without exception, we all benefit from its achievements. God has shown us truths about the physical world through the sciences of chemistry, medicine, electronics and physics. He has taught us about human behavior through the sciences of anthropology, sociology and psychology. For some, however, science has become a god, a religion, and an object of worship. The facts and the methods of science are accepted by these people without question, and they forget that science, like theology, is built upon a set of presuppositions and assumptions that must, like religion, be accepted by faith.

Currently the god of science seems to be declining. Young people are recognizing that while science has enabled man to make tremendous advances, scientific facts are not able to solve man's problems. So young people are turning to a more contemporary idol—the god of political activism. In the 1950s college students were described as unconcerned, uninvolved, and inactive, but in the 1960s they changed. The civil rights movement arose in protest of racial injustice. The anti-war movement gained pre-eminence among those who considered American involvement in Viet Nam wrong. Toward the end of the sixties, student unrest spread throughout campuses of the Western world. Students protested social injustice, impersonal university systems that treated people as numbers on an IBM card, and other world ills. This became a rallying banner for students who otherwise would have had no other purpose for living. These people have ignored the God of Scripture, and their vacuum has been filled by social and political activism.

A fourth idol is the god of experience. Some people today live only for the turned-on feelings that come with sex and drugs. In themselves, of course, there is nothing wrong with either of these. Sex was created by God, sanctioned in Scripture, and called "honorable"[7] when it is the expression of love between a man and his wife. Properly used drugs can relieve pain, cure ills, and calm emotional disturbances. For many people, however, sex has become an obsession and the heightened awareness that comes from drug use is so powerful a god that experience-worshippers are willing to ignore the consequences and yield completely to anything that will bring temporary arousal.

Survival is a fifth god. There is much legitimate concern these days about pollution, overpopulation, and other problems that threaten the existence of our world. Scientific experts have demonstrated effectively that unless drastic changes are made, man will not survive another century on this earth.[8] But ecology can also become an idol which replaces the God of the Scriptures and become an object of worship and persistent concern.

Then there is the tendency for man to become his own god. Some of the statements which were made following the Apollo 11 moon walk came close to human worship. "Clearly man can do anything he sets his mind to," one of the astronauts stated, which is another way of saying that man is omnipotent and omniscient. Modern humanism stresses the capabilities, the pre-eminence and the glory of man. Human achievements are put on a high pedestal and the accomplishments of mankind are widely proclaimed. All of this is inconsistent with the Bible's teaching that man is an imperfect being who has so many failures and conflicts that he is unworthy of being an object of worship.

The seventh god, and one that is gaining great popularity, is the god of occultism. Hundreds of thousands of people are interested in astrology, in horoscopes, in witchcraft, in prophecies of Jean Dixon, in Ouiji boards or in attempts to communicate with the dead. People who dismiss the supernatural features of Christianity readily worship and acknowledge the Satanic principles and powers which we are warned against in the

Bible.[9] In some places, occultism is even coming into the church and people are replacing God with a Satanic idol.

These of course are not the only idols of the twentieth century. Keith Miller has dealt with this very explicitly in his book *The Taste of New Wine.*

> ...ask yourself the question, "What is the most important thing in the world to me?" The temptation is to say, "God," but let me tell you some ways you can tell what is really most important to you. What do you think about again and again when your mind is not engaged with work or with someone else? Let me give you some suggestions of the kinds of things I mean: Do you think about your wife or husband (or children)? Do you think about being great in your vocation? Or being considered a brilliant person? Or socially sophisticated? Or are your recurring thoughts about sex or your own beauty? Or are your thoughts when alone centered in your own problems, jealousy etc....centered in yourself?...
>
> Now each of these thoughts is like a rubber ball on a string tied to the center of your mind. You throw it out and get busy with the work of the day. But when you are alone, back it comes again and again to sit in the middle of the stage of your attention. I am asking you to consider this because whatever you focus this hottest intensity of your mind on is very likely *what you worship instead of Jesus Christ!* For what is worship if it is not the object of your life's most intense focus?
>
> I am not implying that Christ says that it is wrong to love one's children or wife or vocation (or goals). But it is wrong to love them more than God. It is wrong to make idols of them. It ruins them and us.[10]

Dealing with Emptiness

Embracing idols is one way in which modern man deals with this emptiness, but there are other ways. Frankl, for example, has concluded that there are three effective techniques for dealing with the problem.[11] First, he suggests, we should *experience* something like love, joy, curiosity, or humor. Secondly, he believes that *suffering* can bring meaning to our lives, and thirdly, he emphasizes the importance of *activity*— doing a deed, or getting involved in some activity, especially when it helps another person. Other psychologists have suggested that a good hobby or other leisure pastime can be helpful, although most of us have heard of people who, when they are able to devote large amounts of time to their hobbies, have found that both the novelty and interest eventually wears off.

Other people have more success in defeating emptiness by finding challenging work. Musicians and scientists, for example, often find that their vocation is an all-consuming passion which fills their lives. Regretfully, relatively few people have work which is that meaningful, and even for those who do, there are some disturbing questions which keep cropping up (if we let them). Why is my work so important? Where is it all leading? Does my life and work really matter?

Within recent years a number of philosophers, psychologists, and others have been saying that the answer to emptiness is "to grin and bear it." We must learn to live, they suggest, in "meaninglessness." Life doesn't really have any purpose, they tell us; it really *is* empty and meaningless. It is, in the groaning of Macbeth, "a tale told by an idiot, full of sound and fury and signifying nothing." This hopeless attitude doesn't inspire or motivate people. Why bother to get excited about anything, if life is only a meaningless valley between "the cold and barren peaks of two eternities"? For .such people the only goal in life is to "eat, drink and be merry, for tomorrow we die!"

The Biblical Response to Emptiness

In contrast to many modern men, the ancient Word of God does not give a depressing picture of life. Jesus once said He came so that people might have life which they could live abundantly.[12] When he wrote to the Philippians, the Apostle Paul spoke approvingly of life with Christ in the future, but he also talked of an exciting life that was possible here on earth.[13] Certainly Paul's life had problems, frustrations and anxieties, but it also had fruitful labor, joy, purpose, meaning and fulfillment.

There once was a time I used to tell people that the answer to emptiness was faith in Christ. "Believe on the Lord Jesus Christ," I would say, "and you will be saved both from eternal punishment in the future and from emptiness on the earth." This was a nice, simple solution, but it ignored the fact that there are thousands of Christians who believe in Christ but whose lives are empty and without any real purpose.

Why are these modern Christians so different·

from Paul who had such a full life? To find the answer we might look again to Israel in the wilderness. When he discovered the golden calf, Moses broke it in pieces and stood at the gate of the camp where he asked the question. "Who is on the Lord's side? Let him come unto me." [14] Those who didn't come lost their lives. To those who did come, Moses announced "Today you have ordained (set apart) yourselves for the service of the Lord." [15]

For the man who would find meaning in life today, unusual experiences, suffering, finding a hobby, or being involved in a successful vocation can and does give satisfaction, but real fullness comes only when a person completely sets himself apart for the service of Christ. This is explicitly stated in the Book of Romans and again in the Book of Hebrews. "I appeal to you," Paul writes, to "present your bodies as a living sacrifice, holy and acceptable to God, which is your spiritual worship. Do not be conformed to this world, but be transformed by the renewal of your mind, that you may prove what is the will of God, what is good and acceptable and perfect." [16] Then in Hebrews we read, "Let us also lay aside every weight, and sin which clings so closely, and let us run with perseverance the race that is set before us, looking to Jesus. . ." [17]

We learn God's will through the Scriptures, through circumstances (open and closed doors), and through the use of their God-given brains. None of this works, however, unless we first really want God's perfect will for our lives. Not all Christians do. A lot of us prefer to make our own plans and then to get a divine rubber stamp of approval. Others seem to assume that God plays a game in which He says, "I want you to do My will but I'm hiding My plan for your life and you have to find it in a game of hide and seek." But this is not God's way for those who seriously want to serve and follow Christ. If we are yielded, we will find that He will lead.

The God who created the world still holds all things together and gives stability in the time of rapid change. He frees us from emptiness in an age of excessive leisure time, spiritual unbelief, and man-made idols. This is the only real way to avoid emptiness and to find true meaning in life.

Questions for Further Thought and Discussion

1. Do you agree that "the person who has a reason for living and a purpose in life can tolerate almost any difficulty"?
2. Is your life full and meaningful? If not, why not?
3. What are some other reasons for emptiness in people's lives today? Can you think of causes in addition to those listed by the author?
4. In this chapter the author refers frequently to the experience of Israel at Mt. Sinai. What does this have to do with emptiness? Can you think of other Biblical illustrations or references dealing with this issue?
5. Do you think that people really worship idols in the seventies such as those listed in this chapter?
6. What are the idols in your life that keep you from God? Do these give meaning to life? Are they better solutions to the problem of emptiness than are the solutions given in the chapter?
7. What are some successful ways to handle emptiness? What techniques have you used successfully? Are there other ways of meeting the problem that are better than what you are doing?

Footnotes

1. Frankl, V. E. *Man's Search For Meaning: An Introduction to Logotherapy.* New York: Washington Square Press, 1959, pp. 117,120.
2. May, R. *Existential Psychology.* (2nd ed.) *New York:* Random House, 1969.
3. Frankl, V. E. *Psychotherapy and Existentialism: Selected Papers on Logotherapy.* New York: Simon and Schuster, 1967, p. 71.
4. Jess, J. D. *Escape from Emptiness.* Wheaton, Illinois: Tyndale House, 1968, p. 11.
5. Exodus 32.
6. Babbage, S. B. *The Vacuum of Unbelief.* Grand Rapids: Zondervan, 1969.
7. Hebrews 13:4.
8. See Ault, W. V. "Environmental Pollution and Waste of Our Natural and Human Resources," in G. R. Collins (ed.) *Our Society in Turmoil.* Carol Stream, Illinois: Creation House, 1970, pp. 101-110. This book contains articles on a number of other contemporary issues including student unrest, drug abuse, overpopulation, poverty and war.
9. Ephesians 6:12; Isaiah 8:19-22.
10. Miller, K. *The Taste of New Wine.* Waco, Texas: Word Books, 1965, pp. 97-98.
11. Frankl, V. E. *Man's Search for Meaning,* op. cit.
12. John 10:10
13. Philippians 1:21.
14. Exodus 32:25.
15. Exodus 32:29, RSV.
16. Romans 12:1,2, RSV.
17. Hebrews 12:1,2, RSV.